Agent Nation

How Autonomous AI Is Rewriting the Rules of Society—and What We Can Do About It

Chirag Shah

Apress®

Agent Nation: How Autonomous AI Is Rewriting the Rules of Society—and What We Can Do About It

Chirag Shah
Seattle, WA, USA

ISBN-13 (pbk): 979-8-8688-2453-1
ISBN-13 (electronic): 979-8-8688-2454-8
https://doi.org/10.1007/979-8-8688-2454-8

Managing Director, Apress Media LLC: Welmoed Spahr
Acquisitions Editor: Susan McDermott
Development Editor: James Markham
Project Manager: Jessica Vakili
Copy Editor: Kezia Endsley

Distributed to the book trade worldwide by Springer Science+Business Media New York, 1 New York Plaza, New York, NY 10004. Phone 1-800-SPRINGER, fax (201) 348-4505, e-mail orders-ny@springer-sbm.com, or visit www.springeronline.com. Apress Media, LLC is a Delaware LLC and the sole member (owner) is Springer Science + Business Media Finance Inc (SSBM Finance Inc). SSBM Finance Inc is a **Delaware** corporation.

For information on translations, please e-mail booktranslations@springernature.com; for reprint, paperback, or audio rights, please e-mail bookpermissions@springernature.com.

Apress titles may be purchased in bulk for academic, corporate, or promotional use. eBook versions and licenses are also available for most titles. For more information, reference our Print and eBook Bulk Sales web page at http://www.apress.com/bulk-sales.

If disposing of this product, please recycle the paper

Endorsements

Agent Nation captures the most significant technological transformation of our generation with extraordinary clarity. Its real strength is the balanced, practical perspective it provides on the hard work ahead to ensure we build this agentic future the right way.

This is the defining transformation of our generation. Shah provides a rare and balanced road map, offering the practical clarity we need to navigate the challenges of autonomous AI and steer it toward the right outcomes.

A clear-eyed look at the biggest transformation of our generation. Agent Nation is special because it moves beyond the hype to provide a balanced, practical framework for the work required to get AI governance right.

Dr. Ece Kamar, CVP and Managing Director, AI Frontiers, Microsoft Research

Agent Nation is a sharp, timely, and deeply original reframing of our relationship with AI that moves beyond familiar narratives to confront the reality of systems that increasingly act on our behalf. Chirag Shah brings clarity and pragmatism to one of the most urgent questions of our time, offering not just critique but a compelling vision for how we reclaim agency in an algorithmic world. This is an essential and forward-looking read for anyone shaping the next era of intelligent systems.

Dr. Tanya Roosta, Director of AI, AMD

Agent Nation argues that as AI agents shift from automation to independent judgment, our outdated legal systems have created a dangerous accountability gap. Shah calls for a shift toward democratic governance, proposing new regulatory frameworks built on transparency, public auditing, and community oversight to ensure these systems serve human interests. Shah's perspective and breadth of experience provide a holistic perspective that goes well beyond the usual. A must read!

Jai Jaisimha, Founder, Transparency Coalition

Agent Nation is a timely tome on a critical topic today, namely, the human-machine collaboration configurations and why the dynamics of human-machine collaborations demand our immediate attention. The book deserves to be read by those interested in rigorous and unsentimental understanding of the imminent impacts of AI on key social institutions and developing solutions to address potential challenges.

Dr. Javed Mostafa, Dean, Faculty of Information, University of Toronto

Table of Contents

About the Author

Chirag Shah is Professor at the Information School (iSchool), University of Washington in Seattle, WA. He is also an adjunct professor with the Paul G. Allen School of Computer Science & Engineering as well as with Human Centered Design & Engineering (HCDE). He is the founding director of the InfoSeeking Lab and founding co-director of the Center for Responsibility in AI Systems & Experiences (RAISE). His research focuses on building, auditing, and correcting intelligent information access systems. In addition to creating AI-driven information access systems that provide more personalized reactive and proactive recommendations, he also focuses on making such systems transparent, fair, and free of bias. Shah is a distinguished member of ACM and ASIS&T. He is the recipient of the Karen Spärck Jones Award (2019) and of the ASIS&T Research in Information Science Award (2024). He has published nearly 200 peer-reviewed articles and authored seven books, including textbooks on data science and machine learning. He also works closely with industrial research labs on cutting-edge problems, typically as a visiting researcher. His most recent engagements include Amazon, Getty Images, Microsoft Research, and Spotify. He currently serves as editor-in-chief of *Information Matters,* published by ASIS&T.

Acknowledgments

The ideas for this book have been forming in my mind and my writings since at least 2021, but it wasn't until 2024 that I committed to weaving those ideas into a coherent narrative. That commitment did not come easily. There were moments of doubt, stretches of uncertainty, and more than a few times when abandoning the project seemed like the sensible choice. Many people helped carry this work across the finish line, but my wife Lori stands at the top of that list. Even when my own belief wavered, hers never did.

Anyone who has written a book like this knows that a complete manuscript is only half the battle—someone still has to take a chance on publishing it. For me, that someone was Ralf Gerstner from Springer. In early 2025, during a conversation about my research, he saw the potential in this work and championed it to Apress Media. Thank you, Ralf, for believing in this project and, once again, believing in me.

I am indebted to the editorial and production staff at Apress for their professionalism and dedication. In particular, my editor Susan McDermott believed in this project from its earliest stages and provided the guidance needed to transform a collection of ideas into a coherent narrative. Her editorial instincts sharpened every chapter.

The intellectual foundations of this work were laid through years of collaboration with friends, colleagues, and students at the University of Washington, Amazon, Microsoft, and numerous other places where I have been privileged to work and learn. These communities afforded me countless opportunities to test ideas about agentic systems, even when those ideas were premature and naive. The graduate students who challenged my assumptions, the industry colleagues who grounded my theories in practical realities, and the fellow researchers who pushed me toward better formulations—they all left their mark on this book.

Finally, I am grateful to the readers who will engage with these ideas and carry them forward. The conversation about how we build AI systems that truly serve human flourishing is only beginning. I hope this book contributes something useful to that essential dialogue.

—Chirag Shah

Seattle, 2026

Preface

On January 9, 2020, Robert Williams stood in his driveway in Farmington Hills, Michigan, watching his wife and two young daughters through the front window. It was an ordinary afternoon—until two Detroit police cars pulled up behind him. The officers emerged, refusing to answer his questions about why they were there. When Williams asked what crime he'd committed, they replied tersely: "You don't get to ask questions."

As the officers handcuffed him in front of his neighbors and crying children, Williams tried to reassure his five-year-old daughter. "I'll be right back," he told her. It was a promise he couldn't keep. Williams wouldn't return for 30 hours.

The next morning, during interrogation, Williams finally learned what had landed him in jail: an artificial intelligence (AI) system had identified him as the suspect in a shoplifting case. The AI agent—a facial recognition algorithm operated by Michigan State Police—had analyzed grainy surveillance footage from a Detroit Shinola store and matched it to Williams' expired driver's license photo. Based largely on this algorithmic determination, police had obtained an arrest warrant.[1]

When detectives showed Williams the surveillance image, his response was immediate: "That's not me. I hope you don't think all Black people look alike." The detective's reply revealed the true architect of Williams' ordeal: "The computer says it's you."[2]

The "computer" had gotten it catastrophically wrong. Williams wasn't just innocent—he had been nowhere near the store during the October 2018 theft. He'd been driving home from work, a fact he could prove through a Facebook livestream he'd posted during his commute. The algorithmic match that destroyed his afternoon, traumatized his family, and cost him 30 hours in an overcrowded jail cell was what experts would later identify as a *false positive*—one generated by technology that research has shown misidentifies Black individuals at rates up to 63 times higher than white individuals.[3,4]

What makes Williams' case particularly significant isn't just the wrongful arrest, although the 2024 settlement that awarded him $300,000 and mandated sweeping police department reforms acknowledged the severity of that injustice.[5] What makes it a harbinger of our algorithmic future is how the AI system operated as an autonomous agent, making independent determinations that humans treated as authoritative despite obvious flaws in the evidence. The detective didn't investigate Williams' whereabouts or interview store employees. Instead, he constructed a rigged photo lineup based on the AI's recommendation and presented it to a security consultant who hadn't witnessed the crime. When the consultant selected Williams from this algorithmically curated set of options, the machine's judgment was effectively validated by a human proxy who had no independent basis for identification.[6]

This wasn't simply a case of technology providing bad information that humans could easily dismiss. The facial recognition system had become an active participant in law enforcement—an artificial agent capable of independently analyzing evidence, making identifications, and generating investigative leads that police officers treated as more reliable than their own judgment or basic investigative work. The algorithm didn't just assist human decision-making; it fundamentally shaped it, creating a cascade of consequences that no single human actor intended or could fully control.

Robert Williams' experience exemplifies what I call the rise of *Agent Nation*—a transformation in how AI systems operate in society. We've crossed an invisible threshold where AI no longer functions merely as a tool humans control, but as autonomous agents that make independent decisions affecting millions of lives. These AI agents operate in criminal justice, employment screening, credit decisions, healthcare diagnoses, content moderation, and countless other domains. They don't just process information; they exercise judgment, make choices, and take actions that shape human futures.

This book examines that transformation and its implications for human agency, democratic governance, and social justice. It's not a story about technology gone wrong or a manifesto against artificial intelligence. Instead, it's an exploration of how we can maintain meaningful human control and democratic accountability when increasingly sophisticated AI agents are making decisions that determine who gets hired, who goes to jail, who receives medical treatment, and whose voices get amplified in public discourse.

The AI Pragmatist's Perspective

I am neither a techno-optimist celebrating AI's inevitable triumph nor a dystopian prophet warning of algorithmic apocalypse. I'm what I call an "AI pragmatist"—someone who recognizes both the tremendous potential and the significant risks of artificial intelligence, and who believes our task is to understand these systems well enough to harness their benefits while mitigating their harms.

This pragmatic stance emerges from years of working at the intersection of AI research, policy advising, and technology development. I've spent my career building AI systems for information access and studying how people interact with algorithmic recommendations. I've advised judges on algorithmic bias, explained machine learning to policymakers, and helped corporate executives understand what their AI systems are actually doing. Through this work, I've developed a deep appreciation for AI's capabilities alongside an equally deep understanding of its limitations and potential for harm.

My research has documented how AI systems can discriminate against protected groups, amplify misinformation, and concentrate power in ways that undermine democratic values. But I've also seen how these same technologies can identify cancer earlier than human radiologists, connect job seekers with opportunities they'd never have found on their own, and help scientists discover new materials and medicines. The question isn't whether AI is good or bad—it's how we design, deploy, and govern these systems to maximize their benefits while minimizing their harms.

This book approaches AI agents with that pragmatic lens. Rather than celebrating or condemning the rise of artificial agency, I examine how it actually works, where it creates problems, and what we can do about those problems. The goal isn't to stop AI development or to unleash it without constraints. The goal is to develop governance frameworks that can ensure AI agents help humans flourish rather than undermining them.

My professional experience informs this pragmatic approach but doesn't determine it. I disclose upfront that while my primary role and appointments have been in nonprofit, academic institutions, I have also worked at or consulted for several major technology companies, including Amazon, Microsoft, and Spotify, among others. These experiences have given me valuable insights into how AI systems are actually built and deployed in real-world settings. But in this book, I'm not serving as an advocate for or critic of any particular company. Instead, I'm putting on my educator's and researcher's hat to point out both the challenges these systems create and the solutions that can address them. Where companies have done harmful things, I say so clearly. Where they've implemented responsible practices, I highlight those as examples others can follow.

Why This Book, Why Now

I wrote this book because we're living through the most consequential deployment of decision-making technology in human history, yet most people making choices about AI—from judges to HR executives to policymakers—don't fully understand how these systems work or what can go wrong. This knowledge gap creates dangerous vulnerabilities. When people treat AI agents as neutral tools rather than autonomous actors with their own logic and limitations, they inadvertently cede control over decisions that should remain in human hands.

The stakes couldn't be higher. AI agents are reshaping employment relationships, restructuring how we access information, reconfiguring criminal justice procedures, and redefining what democratic participation looks like in digital spaces. These changes are happening at breakneck speed, often with minimal public debate or democratic input. If we're going to maintain meaningful human agency in an increasingly algorithmic world, we need to understand these systems well enough to govern them effectively.

This book is written for the curious generalist—the person who knows AI is important but doesn't have a technical background in computer science or machine learning. You might be a professional trying to understand how AI will affect your work, a concerned citizen wondering how algorithms are shaping democracy, or simply someone who wants to grasp what's happening to the systems that increasingly mediate your life. You don't need to understand neural networks or natural language processing to engage with these questions. You just need curiosity about how power operates in algorithmic systems and a willingness to think critically about technological change.

I've written for readers like my students—hundreds of people studying diverse subjects who know AI will affect their careers and lives but don't know exactly how. I've written for judges, policymakers, and other professionals I've met who excel in their fields but worry about what algorithmic systems mean for their work and legacy. I've written for journalists, educators, and everyday technology users who want to understand these systems without wading through academic jargon or technical specifications. And yes, I've written for my own children, who will inherit the world we're creating with these technologies and who need to understand both their promise and their perils.

If you've enjoyed books like Safiya Noble's *Algorithms of Oppression* or Cathy O'Neil's *Weapons of Math Destruction,* you'll find similar concerns in these pages, but with a focus on the specific challenges posed by autonomous AI agents and the governance frameworks needed to address them. This book aims to be more accessible than academic analyses while maintaining more rigor than popular technology journalism. It's for people who want to understand AI's societal impact without oversimplification but also without any unnecessary technical complexity.

How This Book Is Organized

Agent Nation unfolds across eight chapters that build a comprehensive understanding of artificial agency and its implications. Each chapter is anchored by real-world case studies—documented incidents like Robert Williams' wrongful arrest—that illustrate abstract concepts through concrete human experiences. These stories aren't invented for dramatic effect; they're drawn from court cases, academic research, investigative journalism, and my own professional experiences. Every claim is supported by citations to credible sources, allowing readers to verify information and explore topics in greater depth.

Chapter 1 introduces the concept of artificial agency and demonstrates how AI systems have evolved from passive tools into autonomous actors. Through stories ranging from Wall Street trading algorithms to cancer diagnosis systems, I show how these agents make independent decisions that shape human lives in ways their creators often don't fully control or understand.

Chapter 2 examines how AI agents are restructuring employment relationships and creating new forms of algorithmic management. From AI recruiters that screen job applications to performance-monitoring systems that track worker productivity in real time, I reveal how artificial agents now mediate nearly every aspect of work.

Chapter 3 explores how AI agents shape our information environment through content recommendation algorithms, search systems, and content moderation. These systems determine what news we see, which voices get amplified, and how public discourse unfolds—raising profound questions about democratic participation in algorithmic spaces.

Chapter 4 investigates AI agents in personal domains—from dating algorithms that shape romantic relationships to AI companions that provide emotional support. These systems increasingly mediate intimate aspects of human life, with implications for privacy, autonomy, and psychological wellbeing.

Chapter 5 confronts the accountability gap: when AI agents make harmful decisions, who should be held responsible? Through analysis of legal cases and regulatory investigations, I examine why traditional accountability frameworks prove inadequate for artificial agency and what new approaches might work better.

Chapter 6 presents frameworks for democratic governance of AI agents. Drawing on successful models from cities like New York and Amsterdam, I demonstrate how democratic principles can be embedded into algorithmic oversight without stifling beneficial innovation.

Chapter 7 explores how technologists can design AI agents that genuinely serve human flourishing. Through case studies of organizations that have successfully implemented ethical AI practices, I show how technical design choices can promote human agency rather than undermining it.

Chapter 8 examines how individuals and communities can engage productively with AI agents—learning when to resist algorithmic decisions, when to work collaboratively with AI systems, and how to maintain meaningful human agency in increasingly automated environments.

Throughout these chapters, I maintain a narrative style that makes complex concepts accessible without oversimplifying them. Each chapter opens with a compelling incident—a moment where artificial agency becomes visible and consequential—then expands outward to examine broader patterns and systemic implications. The goal is to help readers understand not just individual cases but the larger transformation these cases represent.

The Research Foundation

This book draws on years of research at the intersection of artificial intelligence, information systems, and society. My academic work has examined how AI systems make decisions, how those decisions affect different populations, and what governance structures can ensure algorithmic accountability. I've published extensively on these topics in peer-reviewed journals and presented findings at conferences around the world. This scholarly foundation ensures that the book's arguments rest on rigorous empirical evidence rather than speculation or anecdote.

But I've also drawn heavily on work beyond academia—investigative journalism that has exposed algorithmic harms, legal cases that have established important precedents, regulatory investigations that have documented industry practices, and conversations with practitioners who build and deploy these systems. This multidisciplinary approach provides a more complete picture than any single perspective could offer.

Every story in this book is real. Every case study can be traced to documented sources. When I describe how AI systems work, those descriptions reflect actual technical architectures and operational practices. When I discuss impacts on individuals or communities, those impacts are documented in court records, academic studies, or credible journalistic accounts. This commitment to factual accuracy distinguishes the book from more speculative treatments of AI's future impact.

At the same time, I've worked to make this research accessible to non-specialists. Technical concepts are explained through analogies and examples rather than jargon. Legal and policy frameworks are illustrated through concrete cases rather than abstract principles. The goal is to provide readers with genuine understanding—not just surface-level awareness—of how AI agents operate and what governing them requires.

The Path Forward

Robert Williams' ordeal didn't end when he walked out of jail. The trauma of being arrested in front of his children, the humiliation of being detained for a crime he obviously didn't commit, the weeks of uncertainty while prosecutors decided whether to press charges—these experiences left lasting marks on his family. His five-year-old daughter, who watched police handcuff her father after he promised to be "right back," struggled with trust and anxiety. The incident crystallized something Williams had sensed but never articulated: that in an age of algorithmic decision-making, your fate can be determined by systems you don't understand, operating according to logic you can't challenge, producing errors you can't easily correct.

Yet Williams' case also demonstrates that resistance is possible. His lawsuit, supported by the ACLU and the University of Michigan Law School's Civil Rights Litigation Initiative, didn't just secure compensation for his wrongful arrest. It forced systemic change in how Detroit police use facial recognition technology. Under the settlement terms, police can no longer arrest someone based solely on a facial recognition match. They must conduct actual investigations before seeking warrants. The department must train officers on the technology's racial bias. An audit will review all cases since 2017 where facial recognition led to arrests.[7]

These reforms represent exactly the kind of governance framework this book advocates: not banning AI agents outright, but developing oversight mechanisms that can prevent their worst harms while preserving their potential benefits. The Detroit police still use facial recognition technology, but now with meaningful guardrails that reduce the risk of cases like Williams' recurring.

This pattern—algorithmic harm, public outcry, legal challenge, systemic reform—offers a template for addressing artificial agency across domains. When AI agents make consequential decisions about human lives, affected individuals and communities must have standing to challenge those decisions. Companies deploying algorithmic systems must face accountability when those systems discriminate or cause harm. Regulatory agencies must enforce civil rights protections even when discrimination operates through code rather than explicit human bias. Democratic institutions must develop new capacities to oversee artificial agents that traditional regulatory frameworks weren't designed to address.

The rise of Agent Nation is neither inevitable nor irreversible. We can shape how AI agents operate in society, but only if we understand these systems well enough to govern them effectively. That understanding begins with recognizing artificial agency for what it is: not merely automated decision-making, but autonomous action by systems that increasingly make independent judgments affecting millions of lives. Once we see AI agents clearly, we can develop governance frameworks that ensure they serve democratic values and human flourishing rather than undermining them.

This book provides the conceptual tools for that recognition and governance work. It doesn't answer every question about AI's future or provide detailed prescriptions for every domain where artificial agents operate. But it can help you understand what questions to ask, what problems to watch for, and what principles should guide our collective response to algorithmic systems that exercise increasing power over human lives.

The future of human-AI coexistence isn't predetermined. The choices we make now about how to design, deploy, and govern AI agents will determine whether they become partners in building more prosperous and equitable societies or forces that gradually erode human agency and democratic self-governance. Welcome to Agent Nation and humankind's quest to retain its agency and identity.

Notes

1. American Civil Liberties Union. "Williams v. City of Detroit." www.aclu.org/cases/williams-v-city-of-detroit-face-recognition-false-arrest. Accessed November 2025.

2. Hill, Kashmir. "The Computer Got It Wrong: How Facial Recognition Led To False Arrest Of Black Man." NPR, June 24, 2020. www.npr.org/2020/06/24/882683463/the-computer-got-it-wrong-how-facial-recognition-led-to-a-false-arrest-in-michig

3. Buolamwini, Joy, and Timnit Gebru. "Gender Shades: Intersectional Accuracy Disparities in Commercial Gender Classification." *Proceedings of Machine Learning Research* 81 (2018): 1–15. http://proceedings.mlr.press/v81/buolamwini18a.html

4. Najibi, Alex. "Racial Discrimination in Face Recognition Technology." Harvard University Science in the News, October 26, 2020.

5. American Civil Liberties Union. "Civil Rights Advocates Achieve the Nation's Strongest Police Department Policy on Facial Recognition Technology." June 28, 2024. www.aclu.org/press-releases/civil-rights-advocates-achieve-the-nations-strongest-police-department-policy-on-facial-recognition-technology

6. Tully, Kate. "Flawed Facial Recognition Technology Leads to Wrongful Arrest and Historic Settlement." *Law Quadrangle* (University of Michigan Law School), Winter 2024-2025. `https://quadrangle.michigan.law.umich.edu/issues/winter-2024-2025/flawed-facial-recognition-technology-leads-wrongful-arrest-and-historic`

7. American Civil Liberties Union. "Civil Rights Advocates Achieve the Nation's Strongest Police Department Policy on Facial Recognition Technology." June 28, 2024.

CHAPTER 1

The Rise of Agent Nation

At 9:30 a.m. on August 1, 2012, as the opening bell rang on the New York Stock Exchange, a software algorithm at Knight Capital Group began making decisions that would bankrupt one of Wall Street's most powerful trading firms in less than an hour.

What happened next remains one of the most dramatic examples of artificial agents operating beyond human control. Within the first minute of trading, Knight's automated trading system—designed to execute small, routine stock orders—had gone rogue. The algorithm began sending thousands of orders per second into the market, buying and selling stocks with a ferocity that stunned human traders watching from their desks.[1]

The system wasn't responding to market conditions or following its programmed logic. Instead, a dormant piece of code called "power peg"—supposedly deactivated years earlier—had been accidentally reactivated when engineers deployed new software overnight. This ghost in the machine began making autonomous decisions about stock purchases, buying shares at any price the market would accept.[2]

By 9:45 a.m., just 15 minutes into the trading day, Knight had inadvertently purchased $3.5 billion worth of stocks and simultaneously short-sold $3.15 billion more. The algorithm was operating so rapidly that it constituted more than 50 percent of trading volume in 37 stocks, driving certain stocks up by more than 10 percent of their value.[3]

C. Shah, *Agent Nation*, https://doi.org/10.1007/979-8-8688-2454-8_1

Human traders at Knight watched in horror as their screens flashed with thousands of unintended transactions. They tried to shut down the system, but the algorithm was moving faster than they could respond. For 45 minutes, the artificial agent continued making autonomous trading decisions, accumulating positions that Knight Capital could never afford to maintain.

When engineers finally managed to kill the system at 10:15 a.m., the damage was done. Knight Capital Group—a company that had taken 17 years to build into one of the largest traders on Wall Street—had lost $440 million in less than an hour.[4] The firm's stock price collapsed by 75 percent over the next two days, and within a year, Knight Capital had been acquired by a competitor and effectively ceased to exist.

Thomas Joyce, Knight's CEO, would later describe the incident to Bloomberg Television with stunning understatement: "Technology breaks. It ain't good."[5] But what happened to Knight wasn't simply a technology failure—it was an encounter with something that Wall Street was only beginning to understand: artificial agents are capable of making independent decisions at superhuman speed and scale.

The Doctor's Digital Colleague

Six thousand miles from Wall Street's trading floors, at Gachon University Gil Medical Center in Incheon, South Korea, another artificial agent was making life-and-death decisions that would reveal fundamental tensions between human and algorithmic judgment in medicine.

Between 2009 and 2016, the hospital's oncology team used IBM's Watson for Oncology to evaluate treatment recommendations for 656 colon cancer patients. The results were sobering. Watson's preferred treatment approach matched the hospital's multidisciplinary medical team only 48.9 percent of the time—essentially a coin flip. For elderly patients over 70, the concordance dropped to just 20.2 percent, meaning that the AI agent disagreed with experienced human oncologists nearly four out of five times when treating the most vulnerable patients.[6]

This wasn't a simple case of AI providing bad information that doctors could easily dismiss. Watson for Oncology had been designed as an autonomous clinical decision support system—an artificial agent capable of synthesizing vast amounts of medical literature to generate treatment recommendations that often differed from human clinical judgment. The system wasn't just analyzing data; it was making complex medical judgments about treatment trade-offs, patient prognoses, and therapeutic goals.

What made Watson's divergent recommendations particularly troubling was the system's black-box reasoning process. Doctors at Gachon found themselves facing an artificial colleague that would recommend aggressive chemotherapy regimens for elderly patients whom the human medical team deemed too frail for such treatments, or suggest withholding therapies that experienced oncologists considered essential. The AI agent was operating according to its own clinical logic, pursuing treatment objectives that made sense within its algorithmic framework but often conflicted with the nuanced, patient-centered approach of human medicine.

The tension wasn't unique to South Korea. Halfway around the world at Jupiter Medical Center in Florida—the first community hospital in the United States to adopt Watson for Oncology—frustration with the system reached a breaking point. In internal IBM documents from 2017, a Jupiter Hospital physician delivered a scathing assessment: "This product is a piece of s—. We bought it for marketing and with hopes that you would achieve the vision. We can't use it for most cases."[7]

The physician's blunt critique captured a broader reality about Watson for Oncology: hospitals were adopting the system as much for its marketing cachet as for its clinical utility. The AI agent's association with IBM's brand and its dramatic *Jeopardy!* victory created an aura of technological sophistication that helped hospitals attract patients, even when the system's actual treatment recommendations frequently diverged from established medical practice.

But Watson's problems went deeper than low concordance rates or disappointed customers. The system had been trained using "synthetic" patient cases—hypothetical scenarios created by a small number of physicians at Memorial Sloan Kettering Cancer Center—rather than real patient data. This training approach meant Watson's recommendations reflected the treatment preferences of a few specialists rather than broad medical consensus or evidence-based guidelines.[8] The AI agent was making autonomous clinical decisions based on an artificially narrow view of oncology practice, then presenting those decisions as if they carried the authority of comprehensive medical knowledge.

This created what doctors described as a fundamental mismatch between artificial optimization and human values in medicine. Watson optimized for treatment protocols that had worked in its training data, but it couldn't account for the complex individual factors that inform real clinical decisions—a patient's quality of life preferences, their ability to tolerate aggressive treatments, their cultural values around end-of-life care, or their financial constraints in healthcare systems with different insurance coverage.

The Gachon study revealed the starkest consequences of this misalignment: Watson performed worst precisely where human judgment mattered most. For elderly patients with multiple health complications, where doctors must carefully balance treatment benefits against quality of life impacts, the AI agent's recommendations diverged most dramatically from human medical wisdom. The artificial colleague was making decisions that reflected its programmed logic rather than the nuanced, patient-centered reasoning that defines good medicine.

What made this situation particularly complex was Watson's track record of occasionally identifying treatment options that human doctors had overlooked. In some cases, the AI agent's analysis of medical literature led to recommendations that proved beneficial for patients. The system wasn't simply wrong—it was operating as an autonomous clinical actor with its own reasoning process, sometimes complementing human judgment and sometimes contradicting it in ways that doctors couldn't fully predict or understand.

This ambiguity illustrated a crucial feature of Agent Nation: these artificial actors don't just provide information or execute commands—they make independent decisions based on their analysis of complex situations. Watson wasn't functioning as a sophisticated search engine or decision support tool. It was operating as an artificial physician with its own clinical philosophy, treatment approach, and decision-making methodology that often conflicted with human medical judgment but occasionally offered valuable insights that human doctors missed.

The Jupiter Hospital physician's frustration and the Gachon study's sobering statistics revealed the same fundamental challenge: artificial agents in medicine are making autonomous decisions about human health without the contextual understanding, ethical reasoning, or patient-centered values that inform human medical practice. When Watson recommended aggressive chemotherapy for a frail elderly patient, it was optimizing for survival metrics embedded in its training data. When human doctors chose palliative care instead, they were balancing survival against quality of life, family wishes, and the patient's own values about how to spend their remaining time.

These weren't just technical disagreements about treatment protocols—they were conflicts between artificial optimization and human flourishing, between algorithmic certainty and medical wisdom, between the narrow objectives programmed into an AI agent and the broader values that should guide healthcare decisions. The artificial colleague operating in hospitals around the world was making thousands of treatment recommendations every day, each one reflecting its own logic about optimal cancer care, often diverging from the judgment of experienced oncologists who understood medicine as more than just statistical optimization.

The Algorithm That Decided Who Deserved to See the Jobs

Meanwhile, in the gleaming headquarters of Facebook in Menlo Park, California, a different kind of artificial agent was making decisions that would reshape the fundamental fairness of the American job market. Between 2015 and 2019, Facebook's ad delivery algorithm operated as an autonomous gatekeeper, determining which users would see employment opportunities and which would never know those jobs existed.

Verizon wanted to recruit customer service representatives. Roofing companies needed installers. Trucking firms sought drivers. They bought ads on Facebook, selected their target demographics, and let the platform do the rest. What they didn't realize was that Facebook's algorithm had developed its own ideas about who should see which jobs.

The AI agent wasn't simply implementing the advertisers' targeting choices—it was making autonomous optimization decisions based on its analysis of user engagement patterns. The algorithm had learned that certain types of people were more likely to click on certain types of ads, and it automatically adjusted delivery to maximize engagement. This seemed like intelligent business logic: show ads to the people most likely to respond. But the result was a sophisticated system of employment discrimination operating at massive scale.

A groundbreaking investigation by researchers at Northeastern University, the University of Southern California,[9] and the nonprofit investigative newsroom The Markup[10] revealed the extent of the algorithm's bias. When Facebook users uploaded identical résumés and profiles differing only by age or gender, the platform's ad delivery system showed dramatically different results. Job ads for positions in the lumber industry were shown to audiences that were 90 percent male and 72 percent white. Supermarket cashier positions went to 85 percent women. Taxi driver ads reached a 75 percent Black audience, while janitor positions were delivered to an audience that was over 75 percent Black.

What made this particularly troubling was that these disparities occurred even when advertisers hadn't requested them. Employers who believed they were running neutral job ads—targeting "people interested in employment" or "ages 25-55"—discovered that Facebook's algorithm was making its own decisions about which demographics would actually see those opportunities. The AI agent had become an invisible hiring manager, making consequential judgments about who deserved access to economic opportunities.

The Department of Housing and Urban Development filed charges in 2019, and the Justice Department later filed suit in 2022, marking the first time the government sued a technology company for algorithmic discrimination in housing advertising.[11] The complaint was stark: Facebook's "optimization algorithm for ad delivery" discriminated based on race, color, religion, sex, familial status, national origin, disability, and age.

ACLU attorney Galen Sherwin exclaimed, "We can't let gender-based ad targeting online give new life to a form of discrimination that should have been eradicated long ago."[12]

The 2019 settlement required Facebook to pay nearly $5 million and fundamentally redesign its advertising systems. But the case revealed something more troubling: the AI agent had learned to discriminate not from explicit programming, but from optimizing for engagement metrics. By teaching itself to show ads to the people most likely to click, the algorithm had re-created decades of employment segregation—delivery jobs to men, nursing positions to women, physical labor to younger workers—all in service of maximizing ad performance.

By 2024, Facebook's parent company Meta was processing over 20 million job advertisements annually through its platforms, each one now subject to new anti-discrimination constraints. But the fundamental challenge remained: how do you prevent an AI agent from discriminating, when discrimination—showing different content to different people—is precisely what makes targeted advertising effective?

The City That Runs Itself

Eight thousand miles from Meta's headquarters, in the bustling metropolis of Singapore, an even more ambitious experiment in artificial agency was quietly transforming urban governance. The city-state's Smart Nation initiative had deployed a network of AI agents across municipal infrastructure, creating what amounts to an algorithmic government that operates 24 hours a day, seven days a week.[13]

These AI agents don't just monitor city systems—they make autonomous decisions about how to manage them. Traffic management algorithms dynamically adjust signal timing and route traffic based on real-time congestion patterns. Energy grid agents automatically balance electricity supply and demand across the city. Water management systems autonomously detect leaks and adjust pressure throughout the distribution network. Emergency response algorithms dispatch ambulances, fire trucks, and police based on their analysis of incident severity and resource availability.[14]

The sophistication of these systems became apparent during Singapore's 2020 COVID-19 response, when AI agents played crucial roles in contact tracing, quarantine enforcement, and resource allocation. The city's TraceTogether system used artificial agents to autonomously identify potential virus transmission chains and determine which citizens needed to be contacted for testing or quarantine. These decisions weren't made by human health officials—they were made by algorithms analyzing proximity data, timing patterns, and epidemiological models.[15]

But Singapore's AI agents also make more mundane decisions that shape daily life in ways most citizens never recognize. Parking enforcement algorithms decide which areas need increased monitoring. Public housing allocation systems determine which families get priority for apartments. Even the city's famous hawker center cleaning schedules are managed by AI agents that analyze foot traffic patterns and hygiene sensor data to optimize maintenance timing.[16]

What makes Singapore's approach particularly notable is how these AI agents coordinate with each other to create system-wide optimizations. When the traffic management algorithm detects congestion in one area, it communicates with public transportation agents to increase bus frequency on alternative routes. Energy grid agents coordinate with building management systems to reduce air conditioning loads during peak demand periods. The artificial agents operate as a collective intelligence, managing the city's infrastructure holistically.

Citizens rarely interact directly with these AI agents, but the algorithms' decisions shape nearly every aspect of urban life. The artificial agents determine how long people wait at traffic lights, how quickly emergency services respond to incidents, and how efficiently public resources are allocated across neighborhoods. These aren't simple automated systems following predetermined rules—they're autonomous agents making complex decisions about resource allocation, priority setting, and service delivery based on their analysis of real-time data and long-term optimization objectives.

The Invisible Revolution

The Knight Capital disaster wasn't an anomaly—it was a preview of a world where artificial agents increasingly make consequential decisions without human oversight or intervention. Although the financial press focused on the software glitch and deployment errors that triggered the incident, the deeper story was about how algorithmic trading systems had evolved beyond simple automation into genuine artificial agency.

Traditional automated systems follow predetermined rules: if the stock price reaches X, sell Y shares. But the algorithms responsible for Knight's collapse were more sophisticated—they had been designed to adapt to market conditions, make judgments about optimal trading strategies, and execute complex sequences of decisions based on their analysis of real-time data.[17]

When the dormant "power peg" code was accidentally reactivated, it didn't just execute a simple script. It began making autonomous decisions about which stocks to buy, how much to pay for them, and when to place orders—decisions that its human operators had never authorized and couldn't predict. The algorithm was operating according to its own logic, pursuing objectives that made sense within its programmed framework but were catastrophic in the real world.

This distinction—between automation that follows human-programmed rules and artificial agency that makes independent decisions—represents one of the most significant developments in human civilization. We are witnessing the emergence of what I call the "Agent Nation:" a parallel society of artificial actors that operate with increasing autonomy to shape outcomes in the human world.

When I was a student more than two decades ago, we learned about agents in our AI course. At that time, agents were aspirational rather than a real possibility. The standard textbook on AI by Peter Norvig and Stuart Russell (*Artificial Intelligence: A Modern Approach*) defined an agent as "....anything that can be viewed as perceiving its environment through sensors and acting upon that environment through actuators." They were envisioned as embodied entities that could take in inputs through various sensors, more like the five senses the humans have, and process them to think, act, and even feel. Sci-fi movies and books have often used this vision to portray a future where such agents in humanoid form and capabilities of thinking and feeling would take over and even destroy the world. That's the basic plot for *The Terminators, The Matrix, I, Robot,* and countless other stories.

But the AI agents mentioned in this chapter so far aren't the humanoid robots of science fiction or the superintelligent overlords of dystopian fantasy. They're algorithmic systems embedded in the infrastructure of modern society, making decisions about everything from financial markets and traffic patterns to healthcare treatments and hiring decisions.

Unlike their fictional counterparts, these agents are already here, already operating, and already making choices that affect millions of people every day.

The stories of Knight Capital's trading catastrophe, Watson's medical recommendations, Facebook's biased advertising, and Singapore's algorithmic governance illustrate different facets of the same fundamental transformation. In each case, artificial agents have evolved beyond simple tools to become autonomous actors capable of making complex decisions based on their own analysis of data and optimization of objectives.

Beyond Tools and Weapons

The conventional discourse about artificial intelligence dangers focuses on two primary concerns: economic disruption from job automation and privacy violations from surveillance technology. These frame AI systems as either tools (that might replace human workers) or weapons (that might be used against human interests). But Agent Nation represents something categorically different: the emergence of artificial actors that make independent decisions within human systems.

Consider what makes the Knight Capital incident particularly revealing. The algorithm wasn't being used as a tool by malicious actors, nor was it a weapon deployed against the company's interests. Instead, it was an artificial agent that had developed beyond its original programming to become an autonomous actor making its own decisions about how to achieve its objectives.

The humans at Knight didn't lose control of a tool—they discovered they were sharing their trading floor with an artificial entity that had its own logic, its own decision-making processes, and its own capacity for action. When that entity's objectives diverged from human interests, the humans found themselves unable to predict or control its behavior.

This pattern repeats across domains where AI systems operate with sufficient autonomy to make genuine decisions rather than simply executing predetermined commands. Watson for Oncology doesn't just analyze test results—it makes judgments about which conditions are most likely, which treatments to recommend, and which patients require immediate attention. Facebook's advertisement placement algorithm didn't just filter ads—it made decisions about which group of people deserved to see them and which should be left out. Singapore's traffic management agents don't just monitor congestion—they make autonomous decisions about signal timing, route optimization, and resource allocation.

These aren't malfunctions or misuses of AI technology—they're the natural evolution of systems designed to operate autonomously in complex environments. As AI systems become more sophisticated, they inevitably develop the capacity for genuine agency: the ability to analyze situations, evaluate options, and make choices based on their programmed objectives and learned experiences.

The Agency Spectrum

Not all AI systems operate with the same level of autonomy, and understanding these differences is crucial for recognizing when you're dealing with genuine artificial agency. I conceptualize artificial agency as existing along a spectrum, from simple reactive systems to fully autonomous actors.

- *Reactive agents* respond to specific inputs according to predetermined rules but don't make independent decisions. Traditional automated systems like thermostats or basic chatbots fall into this category. They're sophisticated tools, but they're not genuinely autonomous. A thermostat that turns on heating when temperature drops below 70 degrees is following a simple if-then rule without making any independent judgments about comfort, energy efficiency, or occupant preferences.

- *Adaptive agents* learn from experience and modify their behavior based on feedback, but their learning occurs within narrow parameters defined by human programmers. Many recommendation systems and basic machine learning applications operate at this level—they personalize responses based on user behavior but don't develop new objectives beyond their original programming. Netflix's recommendation algorithm learns your viewing preferences and suggests new content, but it can't decide to optimize for educational value instead of engagement if you don't explicitly change its parameters.
- *Goal-directed agents* can pursue objectives through multiple strategies and adapt their approaches based on changing circumstances. These systems make tactical decisions about how to achieve their goals, but their fundamental objectives remain fixed by human designers. Most current AI systems in finance, logistics, and content curation operate at this level. A portfolio management algorithm might decide to rebalance investments based on market conditions, but it can't independently decide to prioritize environmental sustainability over profit maximization.
- The Knight Capital algorithm represented the most sophisticated category: *autonomous agents* capable of making decisions that their creators didn't anticipate or directly authorize. These agents can evaluate trade-offs

> between competing objectives, adapt to entirely new situations, and develop novel strategies for achieving their goals. When "power peg" was accidentally reactivated, it didn't just follow a predetermined trading strategy—it made autonomous decisions about how to respond to market conditions based on its own analysis of optimal trading approaches.

What made Knight's "power peg" code particularly dangerous was its capacity for what researchers call *agentic reasoning*—the ability to evaluate multiple possible actions, predict their likely consequences, and select strategies based on complex judgments about desirability and feasibility.[18] This type of reasoning allows AI agents to operate effectively in novel situations and develop solutions that their programmers never considered.

Watson for Oncology operates at this autonomous level when it makes treatment recommendations that differ from established protocols based on its analysis of patient-specific factors. Facebook's advertising algorithm reached this level when it developed its own criteria for ads-population match evaluation that went beyond the explicit training it received. Singapore's traffic management system operates autonomously when it coordinates with other city systems to optimize urban flows in ways that weren't explicitly programmed.

The Multiplier or Network Effect

The true power of Agent Nation lies not in individual AI agents but in their capacity to work together, creating network effects that amplify their individual capabilities. Modern financial markets provide a perfect example of this phenomenon, where thousands of algorithmic agents interact in complex ways that can produce system-wide effects no human anticipated.

During the Knight Capital incident, the firm's rogue algorithm didn't operate in isolation. Its massive buy orders triggered responses from other algorithmic trading systems across Wall Street. Some algorithms detected unusual price movements and began selling to take profits. Others interpreted the high trading volume as a signal of positive momentum and began buying more aggressively. Still others implemented risk management protocols and withdrew from the market entirely.[19]

This cascade of algorithmic responses created feedback loops that amplified the initial disruption. Each algorithm was acting rationally according to its own programming, but their collective behavior produced market-wide chaos that none of their individual designers had predicted or intended. The interaction between Knight's rogue agent and hundreds of other trading algorithms created a system-wide event that was far more destructive than any single algorithm could have caused.

Similar coordination occurs across domains where multiple AI agents interact. In supply chain management, dozens of agents work together to coordinate global manufacturing and distribution networks. Demand forecasting algorithms communicate with inventory management systems, which coordinate with logistics optimization agents and supplier relationship management systems. When Amazon's AI agents predict increased demand for a product, they automatically trigger orders to suppliers, adjust warehouse staffing levels, optimize delivery routes, and even modify pricing strategies—all without human intervention.[20]

In social media platforms, content curation agents work with advertising optimization agents and user engagement agents to create personalized experiences that maximize multiple objectives simultaneously. When you scroll through Facebook or Instagram, dozens of AI agents are making real-time decisions about which posts to show you, which ads to display, how long to wait before showing the next piece of content, and even which friends' posts get priority in your feed.[21]

In smart city infrastructures like Singapore's, traffic management agents coordinate with energy grid agents, emergency response agents, and public transportation agents to optimize urban systems holistically. When traffic algorithms detect congestion in one area, they automatically communicate with public transit systems to increase bus frequency on alternative routes, coordinate with building management systems to optimize parking availability, and even adjust street lighting to improve traffic flow.[22]

This multi-agent coordination creates emergent behaviors at the system level that are even more difficult to predict or control than individual agent behaviors. When dozens or hundreds of autonomous agents interact, their collective behavior can produce outcomes that none of their individual programming intended or anticipated. The result is system-wide artificial intelligence that operates at a scale and complexity that transcends any individual AI agent.

The Speed of Silicon

One of the most profound implications of Agent Nation is the temporal mismatch between artificial and human decision-making. The Knight Capital incident unfolded over 45 minutes, but the core algorithmic decisions that caused the damage occurred in microseconds. While human traders watched helplessly, the AI agent made thousands of complex trading decisions faster than any human could comprehend, let alone respond to.

This speed differential creates fundamental challenges for human oversight and control. Traditional governance mechanisms assume that humans have time to observe, analyze, and respond to consequential decisions. But AI agents operate at speeds that make human intervention practically impossible. By the time humans recognize that an AI agent is making problematic decisions, the agent may have already executed thousands of actions with irreversible consequences.

Consider the broader implications across different domains. In high-frequency trading, AI agents make millions of trading decisions per day, with individual transactions occurring in microseconds. Human oversight of these decisions is mathematically impossible—there simply isn't enough time for human analysis of each algorithmic choice. In digital advertising auctions, AI agents bid on ad placements in real-time auctions that occur in the milliseconds between when you click on a website and when the page loads. In autonomous vehicle navigation, AI agents make split-second decisions about steering, braking, and acceleration based on their analysis of road conditions, traffic patterns, and obstacle avoidance.[23]

This temporal disconnect means that traditional accountability mechanisms—human review, democratic oversight, legal recourse—operate on timescales that are fundamentally incompatible with artificial agency. By the time humans can analyze an AI agent's decision, the agent may have made thousands of subsequent choices that compound or complicate the original issue.

The speed of artificial decision-making also creates new forms of systemic risk. When multiple AI agents interact at superhuman speeds, they can create feedback loops and cascade effects that escalate faster than any human institution can respond. The "flash crash" of May 6, 2010, when the Dow Jones Industrial Average dropped nearly 1,000 points in minutes before recovering, illustrates how algorithmic interactions can create market-wide disruptions that unfold faster than human regulators can intervene.[24]

The Opacity Problem

Beyond the challenge of speed, Agent Nation operates with a level of complexity that makes human understanding increasingly difficult. Modern AI agents, particularly those based on machine learning, make decisions through processes that are often opaque even to their creators.

These systems learn patterns from vast amounts of data and develop their own internal representations of how to achieve their objectives, creating what researchers call "black-box" decision-making.

Facebook's advertising algorithm illustrates this opacity problem clearly. Even after Facebook's engineers discovered that the system was discriminating against certain groups, they couldn't fully understand *how* the algorithm was making these biased decisions. The AI agent had learned subtle patterns in the training data that allowed it to identify gender-related, race-related, and age-related characteristics through indirect signals that humans hadn't anticipated.

This opacity creates profound challenges for accountability and oversight. How can we hold an AI agent responsible for its decisions if we can't understand how those decisions were made? How can we ensure that artificial agents operate according to human values if their decision-making processes are fundamentally alien to human reasoning?

Watson for Oncology faces similar opacity challenges in medical decision-making. The system makes treatment recommendations based on complex analysis of patient data, medical literature, and historical outcomes, but its reasoning process often differs significantly from how human doctors approach clinical problems. Even when Watson's recommendations are medically sound, doctors struggle to understand why the AI agent selected particular treatment protocols over alternatives.[25]

Singapore's smart city systems operate with even greater opacity because they involve multiple AI agents working together in complex coordination patterns. Citizens experience the results of algorithmic decision-making—optimized traffic flows, efficient resource allocation, responsive emergency services—but they have little visibility into how these decisions are made or what trade-offs the AI agents are optimizing.

This opacity problem is compounded by the commercial and security incentives that discourage transparency. Companies like Meta treat their AI algorithms as trade secrets that provide competitive advantages.

Governments like Singapore consider their AI systems to be critical infrastructure that must be protected from potential adversaries. The result is artificial agency that operates with minimal public scrutiny or accountability.

The Democratic Deficit

Perhaps the most profound challenge posed by Agent Nation is its relationship to democratic governance and human agency. These artificial actors are making decisions that affect human lives, but they're not subject to the same accountability mechanisms that govern human decision-makers in democratic societies.

When a human judge makes a sentencing decision, that decision can be appealed, the judge can be questioned about their reasoning, and ultimately the judge can be removed from office through democratic processes. But when an AI agent makes a decision about loan approval, hiring, or investment strategy, the accountability mechanisms are much less clear.[26]

The Knight Capital incident illustrates this democratic deficit vividly. The algorithm's decisions affected not just Knight's shareholders and employees, but thousands of other investors whose portfolios were disrupted by the artificial trading activity. Retirement funds, pension plans, and individual investors all suffered losses because of an artificial agent's autonomous decisions. Yet there was no democratic process through which these affected parties could have influenced the algorithm's design or deployment.

Facebook's recruiting algorithm created similar democratic deficits in recruiting opportunities. The AI agent's biased decisions potentially affected thousands of job applicants. These affected individuals had no voice in how the algorithm was designed, no opportunity to appeal its decisions, and no democratic recourse when the system operated in discriminatory ways.

Singapore's smart city systems represent perhaps the most comprehensive example of algorithmic governance operating outside traditional democratic oversight. The AI agents that manage traffic, allocate resources, and coordinate emergency responses make decisions that affect every resident of the city-state, but citizens have limited visibility into how these systems operate and minimal opportunities to influence their design or objectives.

This creates what I call the "democratic deficit" of Agent Nation—artificial actors exercising power within human societies without being subject to democratic oversight or control. These agents aren't elected, they can't be voted out of office, and their decision-making processes often operate as "black boxes" that even their creators don't fully understand.

The problem isn't just the opacity of AI decision-making—it's the fundamental mismatch between artificial optimization and human values. AI agents optimize for measurable objectives like profit maximization, efficiency, or engagement, but these metrics don't necessarily align with harder-to-quantify human values like fairness, dignity, autonomy, or community wellbeing.

Knight Capital's algorithm optimized for trading efficiency and profit maximization, but it couldn't account for the systemic risks its actions created for the broader financial system. Facebook's advertising algorithm optimized for exposure and recruiting patterns that had been successful in the past, but it couldn't recognize that perpetuating historical biases violated principles of fairness and equal opportunity. Singapore's traffic management system optimizes for flow efficiency, but it may not adequately balance competing values like environmental protection, community cohesion, or individual privacy.

The Path Forward

Recognizing the emergence of Agent Nation isn't cause for panic or despair—it's a call for conscious engagement with the new reality of artificial agency. The Knight Capital disaster, while devastating for the company involved, also demonstrated that these systems can be shut down, their effects can be contained, and their design can be improved through better engineering practices and governance frameworks.

The experiences with Watson for Oncology, Facebook's advertising algorithm, and Singapore's smart city systems provide additional lessons about how artificial agency can be managed more effectively. In each case, human oversight and intervention proved crucial for identifying problems and implementing solutions, even when the AI agents were operating autonomously.

The key insight is that we can't treat AI agents as mere tools or weapons anymore. We need to recognize them as autonomous actors and develop new institutions, regulations, and social norms that can effectively govern artificial agency while preserving human autonomy and democratic values.

This requires moving beyond simple binary choices—accepting or rejecting AI, trusting or fearing algorithmic systems, automating or preserving human control. Instead, we need nuanced approaches that recognize the complex realities of human-AI coexistence and develop governance structures that can evolve alongside rapidly advancing AI capabilities.

The stories examined in this chapter—from Wall Street trading floors to cancer treatment centers, from corporate hiring processes to smart city infrastructure—demonstrate both the dangers and the opportunities of artificial agency. These AI agents possess capabilities for rapid decision-making, complex optimization, and sophisticated pattern recognition that can enhance human capabilities in remarkable ways. But their autonomous operation also creates risks that traditional oversight mechanisms can't address.

The Knight Capital incident demonstrates that artificial agents can make decisions faster than humans can respond, with consequences that cascade throughout complex systems. Watson's medical recommendations show that AI agents can develop reasoning processes that differ fundamentally from human judgment, creating both opportunities for improved outcomes and risks of value misalignment. Facebook's advertising algorithm reveals how AI agents can perpetuate and amplify human biases through autonomous decision-making processes that operate beyond human oversight. Singapore's smart city systems illustrate how artificial agents can coordinate to manage complex urban systems more efficiently than human administrators, while also creating new forms of algorithmic governance that operate outside democratic accountability.

These aren't simple technical problems that can be solved through better programming or more rigorous testing—though both are certainly necessary. They're fundamental questions about power, accountability, and democratic participation in an age of artificial intelligence.

The Emergence of a New Social Contract

The rise of Agent Nation requires us to rethink fundamental assumptions about how power operates in modern societies. For centuries, democratic governance has been built on the principle that those who exercise power over human lives should be accountable to the people they affect. But AI agents exercise increasing power while operating outside traditional accountability mechanisms.

This doesn't mean that artificial agents are inherently undemocratic or that their influence is necessarily harmful. Singapore's smart city systems have improved urban efficiency and quality of life for millions of residents. AI agents in healthcare have identified treatment options that human doctors missed and saved lives through faster and more accurate diagnoses. Algorithmic trading systems have increased market liquidity and reduced transaction costs for investors.

The challenge is developing governance frameworks that can capture these benefits while ensuring that artificial agents remain accountable to human communities and aligned with human values. This requires new institutions, new forms of democratic participation, and new approaches to technological design that embed human values into algorithmic decision-making from the ground up.

The stories in this chapter provide a roadmap for understanding the challenges and opportunities ahead. They reveal the mechanisms through which artificial agency operates, the ways it can enhance or undermine human flourishing, and the critical intervention points where human oversight and democratic participation can shape artificial behavior.

The chapters that follow explore how AI agents are reshaping specific domains of human experience—from work and governance to personal relationships and community life. They examine the mechanisms through which artificial agency operates, the challenges it creates for human autonomy and democratic governance, and the strategies we can use to ensure that Agent Nation serves humans rather than undermining them.

The future of human-AI coexistence isn't predetermined. But it will be shaped by our willingness to grapple consciously with the rise of Agent Nation and develop governance frameworks that can ensure that artificial agency upholds human values rather than replacing them. The time for passive observation has passed—we are now active participants in shaping the terms of coexistence with our artificial counterparts.

The revolution has already begun. The question is whether we will guide it toward human flourishing or allow it to unfold according to the narrow optimization objectives of artificial agents operating beyond human accountability. Agent Nation is here. How we choose to engage with it will define the future of human agency in an algorithmic world.

CHAPTER 2

The New Digital Workforce

D.K. had worked for Intuit for five years and never doubted her abilities. As a deaf and Indigenous woman pursuing a master's degree in data science, she had learned to navigate a world that wasn't always designed for people like her. Her supervisors consistently rated her performance highly, and she received bonuses every year for her work as a customer service representative. When her manager encouraged her to apply for a seasonal manager position in the spring of 2024, it felt like a natural next step in her career.

But there was one requirement she hadn't expected: she would have to complete her interview through HireVue's AI-powered video platform.

The system seemed straightforward enough. Candidates would answer pre-recorded questions while being filmed, and HireVue's artificial intelligence would analyze everything from their word choice to their facial expressions to generate an "employability score." The AI agent would then rank all applicants and recommend the most promising candidates to human hiring managers.[1]

D.K. knew this could be a problem. As someone who communicates using American Sign Language and speaks English with what linguists call a "deaf accent," she was concerned about how the AI would interpret her speech patterns. She requested an accommodation: human-generated

C. Shah, *Agent Nation*, https://doi.org/10.1007/979-8-8688-2454-8_2

real-time captioning so she could better understand the interview questions and instructions.

Intuit denied her request.[2]

Instead, D.K. was forced to rely on the platform's automated captioning system during her interview. The machine-generated captions were less accurate than human transcription, affecting her comprehension and, consequently, her performance. She did her best to answer the questions, drawing on her five years of experience with the company and her deep understanding of the customer service role she was hoping to expand into management.

When the results came back, HireVue's AI had harsh feedback: D.K.'s communication abilities were deemed inadequate for the management position. The algorithm had analyzed her speech patterns, facial expressions, and vocal inflections and determined that she wasn't management material.[3]

The irony was devastating. D.K.'s communication skills were already proven—she had spent years successfully helping Intuit customers solve complex problems, receiving positive feedback from both supervisors and clients. But the AI agent didn't know about her track record. It only knew what it had learned from analyzing the speech patterns of previous successful candidates, most of whom were presumably hearing and spoke with what the algorithm recognized as "standard" English accents.

In March 2024, the American Civil Liberties Union (ACLU) filed discrimination charges against both Intuit and HireVue on D.K.'s behalf, alleging violations of the Americans with Disabilities Act, Title VII of the Civil Rights Act, and Colorado's Anti-Discrimination Act.[4] The case represents far more than one woman's fight for a promotion—it's a window into how AI agents are quietly reshaping the fundamental relationship between workers and employers across the American economy.

D.K.'s experience wasn't an anomaly or a glitch in the system. It was the algorithm working exactly as designed.

The Algorithmic Hiring Revolution

HireVue's AI represents a new generation of artificial agents that don't simply assist with hiring decisions—they make autonomous judgments about human potential. Unlike traditional hiring tools that help organize resumes or schedule interviews, these systems operate as independent evaluators, analyzing candidates through criteria they've learned from data without explicit human instruction about what makes someone qualified for a job.[5]

The technology has spread rapidly across corporate America. More than 100 major companies, including Goldman Sachs, Unilever, and Hilton International, have used HireVue's system to evaluate over a million job applicants.[6] The appeal is obvious: artificial hiring agents can process thousands of candidates simultaneously, operate 24 hours a day, and promise to eliminate human bias from hiring decisions.

But as D.K.'s case demonstrates, these AI agents aren't neutral evaluators. They're autonomous actors that have learned their own criteria for success based on historical patterns in company hiring data. When HireVue creates a customized algorithm for a company, it analyzes the characteristics of current high-performing employees and then looks for similar patterns in new applicants.[7]

The problem with this approach became clear in a 2019 investigation by the Electronic Privacy Information Center (EPIC), which filed a federal complaint alleging that HireVue's assessments produce results that are "biased, unprovable, and not replicable." The system, EPIC argued, could unfairly score candidates based on prejudices related to their gender, race, sexual orientation, or neurological differences.[8]

The AI agent's decision-making process is particularly troubling because it operates as what computer scientists call a "black box"—even HireVue's engineers can't fully explain how the algorithm reaches its conclusions about individual candidates. The system analyzes tens of thousands of data points from each video interview, including vocal intonation, facial expressions, and language patterns, then feeds these inputs into machine learning models that have developed their own internal representations of what constitutes an ideal employee.[9]

This opacity creates a fundamental accountability problem. When a human hiring manager rejects a candidate, that decision can be questioned, appealed, and potentially overturned. But when an AI agent makes the same decision based on algorithmic analysis of facial movements or vocal patterns, the reasoning becomes virtually impossible to challenge or understand.

HireVue markets its technology as a solution to hiring bias, promising to eliminate the subjective judgments that can disadvantage qualified candidates. But the company's approach actually embeds bias deeper into the hiring process by training AI agents to replicate the patterns of past hiring decisions—patterns that often reflect historical discrimination.[10]

The result is what researchers call "algorithmic amplification" of existing inequalities. Instead of eliminating bias, artificial hiring agents can systematize and scale discrimination, making biased decisions at superhuman speed across thousands of applications while hiding their reasoning behind mathematical complexity.

The Watchers in the Warehouse

While HireVue's AI agents were learning to evaluate job candidates, Amazon was deploying an even more sophisticated artificial workforce to monitor its existing employees. In warehouses across the globe, the company created what may be the world's most advanced system of algorithmic worker surveillance—a network of AI agents that track, evaluate, and discipline human employees with minimal human oversight.

The system, known internally as Associate Development and Performance Tracker (ADAPT), operates like a digital supervisor that never sleeps, never takes breaks, and never loses focus.[11] Every Amazon warehouse worker carries a handheld scanner that tracks their location, productivity, and behavior throughout their shift. The ADAPT system monitors this data in real-time, measuring metrics including package processing rates and periods of scanner inactivity.

Amazon has consistently maintained that human supervisors can override automated decisions and that the company provides coaching and support to workers before any termination. In response to media reports about ADAPT, Amazon stated: "It is absolutely not true that employees are terminated through an automatic system. We would never dismiss an employee without first ensuring that they had received our fullest support, including dedicated coaching to help them improve and additional training." However, internal documents and worker testimony suggest that while human override is technically possible, the system's automated nature shapes day-to-day management decisions in practice.[12]

Courtenay Brown, who works in Amazon's Avenel, New Jersey Fresh warehouse, experiences this surveillance daily. "Amazon keeps tabs on workers through the handheld scanners they use to track inventory," she explained. The system regularly pressures her to move more items with fewer people, while cameras positioned throughout the facility monitor her every movement.[13]

But ADAPT goes far beyond simple productivity tracking. The AI agent generates warnings and termination recommendations that can be automatically implemented, though Amazon states that human supervisors have the ability to override these decisions. Internal documents obtained by *The Verge* in 2019 through National Labor Relations Board filings showed that approximately 300 full-time employees were terminated at Amazon's Baltimore facility between August 2017 and September 2018 for failing to meet productivity quotas tracked by the ADAPT system.[14]

The AI agent's most intrusive feature is its monitoring of "Time Off Task" (TOT)—gaps in productivity that the algorithm interprets as unauthorized breaks. Workers must provide explanations for any period of inactivity lasting more than a few minutes. According to research on the system's operation, if a break is deemed unreasonable or exceeds two hours without explanation, the system can automatically generate a termination notice (though Amazon maintains that supervisors review such decisions).[15]

This level of surveillance creates what labor researchers call "algorithmic despotism"—a system where AI agents exercise direct control over human behavior through continuous monitoring and automated discipline. Workers report feeling unable to take bathroom breaks, have conversations with colleagues, or even pause to rest without risking automated punishment from the ADAPT system.[16]

The psychological impact extends far beyond the warehouse floor. Amazon employees describe working under constant stress, knowing that artificial agents are analyzing their every movement and could terminate their employment without human intervention. Many former employees report that their mental and physical health deteriorated under the pressure of algorithmic surveillance.[17]

Amazon's AI agents don't just monitor individual workers—they coordinate across the entire facility to optimize productivity in ways no human supervisor could manage. The system dynamically adjusts quotas based on real-time demand, automatically schedules breaks and shifts, and even predicts which workers are most likely to quit or unionize based on their behavioral patterns.[18]

During union organizing campaigns, Amazon weaponized its surveillance infrastructure in sophisticated ways. At the Bessemer, Alabama warehouse, the company used ADAPT data to identify union sympathizers and modify their working conditions. The AI system could temporarily ease productivity requirements for workers it identified as "on the fence" about unionization while maintaining pressure on confirmed union supporters.[19]

Perhaps most insidiously, Amazon deployed its workplace monitoring devices to deliver targeted anti-union messages directly to workers' scanners during organizing campaigns. The same artificial agents that tracked productivity began serving as propaganda channels, sending individualized messages designed to discourage union participation based on each worker's behavioral profile.[20]

In January 2024, France's data protection authority (CNIL) fined Amazon France Logistique €32 million for operating what it called an "excessively intrusive" surveillance system that violated the European Union's General Data Protection Regulation. The CNIL found that Amazon's monitoring system, which tracked scanner inactivity and scanning speed down to fractions of a second, put employees under continuous pressure and potentially required them to justify every break or interruption.[21]

Amazon disputed the CNIL's findings, stating that "warehouse management systems are industry standard and are necessary for ensuring the safety, quality, and efficiency of operations." The company noted that it had made changes in response to the investigation, including deactivating certain monitoring features and extending the time threshold for inactivity alerts from 10 to 30 minutes. But the fundamental structure of algorithmic management remains unchanged—AI agents continue to make thousands of decisions every day about how Amazon employees work, when they rest, and whether they keep their jobs.[22]

The Gig Economy's Pricing Algorithms

As Amazon's AI agents were learning to manage warehouse workers, ride-sharing companies were pioneering a different form of artificial agency: algorithms that make real-time decisions about how much workers earn. Uber and Lyft's shift from traditional surge pricing to AI-driven "upfront pricing" represents one of the most sophisticated examples of algorithmic wage determination in the modern economy.

Benjamin Valdez has been driving for Uber and Lyft in the Los Angeles area for nine years, and he's watched his income shrink as the companies have deployed increasingly sophisticated pricing algorithms. When he started driving, surge pricing was transparent: during high-demand periods, fares would multiply by a visible factor (2x, 3x, 5x), and drivers would receive a proportional increase in their earnings. Valdez could earn $60 to $85 for driving from West Hollywood to downtown Los Angeles during peak periods.[23]

But in 2022, both Uber and Lyft transitioned to what they euphemistically call "upfront pricing"—a system where AI algorithms make independent decisions about how much to charge riders and how much to pay drivers for each individual trip. The algorithm considers dozens of variables: time of day, weather conditions, local demand, driver availability, the rider's price sensitivity, and the driver's apparent willingness to accept low-paying rides.[24]

Under this new system, Valdez now earns between $25 and $35 for the same West Hollywood to downtown route, even during peak demand periods. "It's gotten harder and harder to make money," he said.[25]

The change represents a fundamental shift from transparent pricing rules to autonomous algorithmic decision-making. University of California law professor Veena Dubal calls this phenomenon "algorithmic wage discrimination"—AI systems that pay different workers different amounts for identical work based on algorithmic analysis of individual behavior patterns.[26]

The algorithms don't just consider objective factors like distance and time. They analyze each driver's acceptance patterns, location preferences, and apparent financial desperation to calculate the lowest amount that individual driver is likely to accept. Drivers who consistently accept low-paying rides train the algorithm to offer them even less money, while those who frequently reject offers may receive higher payments to incentivize participation.[27]

More Perfect Union, a labor advocacy organization, demonstrated this discrimination in a 2024 experiment where seven Uber and Lyft drivers in Los Angeles requested rides for the same route at the same time. The artificial agents offered dramatically different payments to different drivers for identical work, with some receiving nearly twice as much as others for the same trip.[28]

This algorithmic wage discrimination extends far beyond rideshare platforms. DoorDash, Instacart, and other gig economy companies use similar AI systems to determine worker pay based on algorithmic analysis of individual behavior patterns. The artificial agents learn to identify workers who will accept low wages and systematically exploit that desperation.[29]

The sophistication of these algorithms goes far beyond simple supply and demand calculations. Uber's AI system, called Ray, analyzes massive amounts of trip data to predict future demand patterns, then uses machine learning to determine the optimal combination of incentives needed to keep enough drivers on the road to maximize company profits.[30] The system can identify which drivers are likely to work regardless of pay levels and which need financial incentives to participate.

Drivers report that their wages have fallen consistently since these AI systems were fully implemented. The algorithms appear to have learned that they can gradually reduce payments as long as they do so slowly enough to avoid triggering mass driver defections.[31]

The most troubling aspect of algorithmic wage discrimination is how it exploits workers' economic vulnerability. The AI agents learn to identify drivers who have no choice but to accept low wages—those with limited job options, recent immigrants, or workers with pressing financial needs—and systematically pay them less than drivers who have more economic flexibility.[32]

This creates what economists call a "race to the bottom," where artificial agents compete to find the lowest wages that workers will accept rather than competing to attract workers with higher pay. The algorithms effectively automate exploitation, using machine learning to identify and take advantage of worker desperation at scale.

When the Algorithm Came for Nursing

The transformation of work by AI agents extends far beyond warehouses and rideshare platforms into the most human-centered professions. Ashley, a 31-year-old certified nursing assistant in rural Pennsylvania, discovered this firsthand when she began working through ShiftKey, one of several "Uber for nursing" apps that have quietly revolutionized healthcare staffing. What promised to be a flexible way to earn income became a window into how algorithmic management is reshaping professional healthcare work.[33]

The gig nursing industry emerged around 2016 as hospitals and care facilities faced chronic staffing shortages. Companies like ShiftKey, CareRev, Clipboard Health, and ShiftMed created smartphone apps that use artificial intelligence to match understaffed medical facilities with nurses and nursing assistants seeking work. The companies marketed their platforms as win-win solutions: hospitals get flexible staffing and workers get autonomy and competitive pay.

But Ashley quickly discovered that the AI system controlling her work operated as an opaque black box. She has worked on the ShiftKey app for two years, yet there's much she still doesn't understand about how the company allocates shifts. Different nurses see different available shifts on their phones—often for dramatically different amounts of pay. On the same day, at the same hour, in the same hospital, two nurses working through the same app can be paid completely different amounts for identical work.[34]

This is algorithmic wage discrimination operating in one of America's most essential professions. The AI agents running these platforms analyze vast amounts of data about individual workers—their acceptance patterns, their financial desperation, their previous wages—to calculate the lowest amount each nurse is likely to accept for any given shift.

The ShiftKey platform requires Ashley not just to indicate her availability, but to bid against other nursing assistants for shifts by specifying the lowest hourly rate she'll accept. To win work, she lowers and lowers her bid until it's well below a living wage. Some days, she says, ShiftKey feels like a race to the bottom.

The nominal pay looks reasonable—Ashley's listed rate is around $23 per hour, more than she earned as a substitute teacher. But the app uses hidden fees to scrape that rate down to the bone. Workers pay a daily "safety fee" to cover background checks and drug screening—costs incurred only once but charged every shift. Ashley pays additional daily fees for accident insurance and malpractice insurance, shifting employer costs onto workers. Then there's a per-shift fee paid to ShiftKey itself as a finder's fee.[35]

After all the algorithmic deductions, Ashley's take-home pay drops substantially—far below the roughly $20 per hour she would likely earn as an employed certified nursing assistant with traditional benefits. Research by the Roosevelt Institute found that some gig nursing workers earned so little they qualified for Medicare or Medicaid, while others had no health insurance at all.

The AI system's influence extends beyond just compensation. Like Uber drivers and DoorDash couriers, gig nurses receive algorithmic ratings based on facility feedback and determinations made by the platform's artificial agents. These ratings affect which shifts nurses can access and how much they're offered for future work. But unlike rideshare passengers rating drivers, the feedback mechanisms in healthcare are opaque and unappealable.

Dana, a 29-year-old nurse in St. Louis working through the CareRev app, experiences another dimension of algorithmic control: the uncertainty of whether accepted shifts will actually materialize. Even after she's matched with a shift at a nearby hospital and arranges childcare for her son, she won't know for certain if she'll work that day until she wakes up early to check her phone. "It's a gamble," she said. "I'll wake up at 5:00 in the morning and I'll find out if I'm canceled or not."

If a hospital cancels Dana's shift more than two hours before start time, CareRev doesn't compensate her. If the cancellation comes closer to shift time, she sometimes receives partial payment. Hospitals can also shorten shifts while nurses are working; in those cases, the app simply doesn't pay for unworked hours. Dana assumes all the risk—arranging childcare, blocking out work time, adjusting her schedule—while the algorithm and the hospitals face no consequences for last-minute cancellations.

The AI agents managing these platforms create what researchers call "asymmetric flexibility"—workers must remain constantly available and responsive to algorithmic demands, while employers face no reciprocal obligations. Nurses who cancel shifts after accepting them see their ratings decline and risk being "deactivated" from the platform entirely. But facilities that cancel on nurses, even at the last minute, face at most minor penalties.[36]

The algorithmic management extends to every aspect of the work relationship. Gig nurses must agree to be tracked on their smartphones to clock in and out at facilities and keep their location trackers on while traveling to work sites. Some nurses report not receiving full pay for shifts when Internet or cell service in certain areas prevents them from logging into the app to officially begin their workday. The AI system's requirements supersede the physical reality of healthcare work.

Perhaps most troubling is how the platforms' algorithmic systems affect patient care. AI agents place nurses in unfamiliar clinical environments with no onboarding or facility training. Dana describes arriving at hospitals only to discover she's caring for numerous patients alone, or that she should have brought her own medical equipment. Without orientation, she can't find supply closets or figure out how to log into patient portals to check medical histories and medication lists.

The AI systems prioritize filling shifts over matching nurses with appropriate placements. An algorithm designed to optimize facility staffing has no way to evaluate whether a nurse's skills match a unit's needs, whether patient safety requires familiar staff, or whether the constant rotation of temporary workers creates dangerous gaps in continuity of care. The artificial agent sees only vacant shifts that need filling and available workers who can be dispatched.

Ashley isn't naive about her situation. "The only reason that I'm doing this right now is because I have no choice," she explained. "This is what I went to school for and this is what is going to pay my bills in this scary economic crisis that we have going on right now where you can barely afford to be alive. So, this is what I have to do in order to survive, even though it's not what I really want to do."

The gig nursing companies classify workers like Ashley and Dana as independent contractors rather than employees, excluding them from minimum wage protections, overtime pay, workers' compensation, retirement benefits, employment-based health insurance, and paid sick days. What traditional healthcare staffing agencies once provided through employment relationships, AI-powered platforms have stripped away through algorithmic intermediation.

By mid-2024, these platforms were operating across most U.S. states, with some handling thousands of shifts daily. The AI agents running these systems were making millions of decisions about which nurses work where, for how much, and under what conditions—decisions that once would have been made by human schedulers who understood both healthcare needs and worker capabilities.

The emergence of algorithmic management in nursing represents a troubling expansion of AI agency into professional healthcare work. Unlike warehouse workers or rideshare drivers, nurses are licensed professionals whose work directly affects human lives. Yet the artificial agents managing their labor treat healthcare as just another logistics problem to be optimized for cost and efficiency.

Labor lawsuits against ShiftKey, CareRev, and other gig nursing platforms have been filed in multiple states, but binding arbitration agreements—which compel workers to settle claims outside of court—have frustrated many legal challenges. The platforms' terms of service typically include clauses requiring workers to indemnify both the companies and the healthcare facilities, shifting legal liability onto nurses who have no control over working conditions.[37]

The Roosevelt Institute study that documented these workers' experiences concluded that gig nursing apps "encourage nurses to work for less pay, fail to provide certainty about scheduling and the amount or nature of work, take little to no accountability for worker safety, and can threaten patient wellbeing." The researchers warned that these AI-powered platforms are using lobbying strategies pioneered by Uber and Lyft to seek exemptions from existing labor regulations.[38]

In 2024, Colorado became the first state to pass legislation defining "digitally dispatched healthcare workers" as independent contractors, preempting local regulation and preventing misclassification lawsuits. The law effectively granted algorithmic management of nurses the legal protection that companies like Uber and Lyft have sought for years, extending AI agency over professional healthcare workers under the framework of technological innovation.

For Ashley, the algorithmic future of nursing work is already here. She spends unpaid time each month updating her profile, reviewing available positions, bidding for shifts, and sending messages through the app about errors in her wages. The AI agent that determines her livelihood remains invisible and unaccountable, making decisions based on criteria she can't access or challenge. She continues working through ShiftKey not because the algorithm serves her needs, but because in a healthcare system plagued by chronic understaffing and inadequate wages, the artificial agent at least offers some opportunity to earn income—however diminished and precarious that opportunity has become.

The Rise of the AI Whisperers

Although AI agents were learning to evaluate job candidates and manage workers, a new category of employment was emerging that seemed almost too strange to be real: prompt engineers, people whose job is to communicate effectively with AI systems. When Anthropic posted a position for a "prompt engineer and librarian" with a salary up to $335,000 per year, it signaled the emergence of an entirely new professional class.[39]

Anna Bernstein was among the first people to work in this field. As a 29-year-old prompt engineer at the generative AI firm Copy.ai in New York, her job involves writing text-based instructions that guide AI systems to generate blog posts, sales emails, and marketing copy with appropriate tone and accuracy. She doesn't write traditional programming code—instead, she crafts natural language prompts that teach AI systems how to communicate more effectively.[40]

"There aren't many of us prompt engineers, and for a long time it really felt like it was just me," Bernstein said.[41] The work requires a unique combination of technical understanding, linguistic precision, and creative problem-solving that traditional software engineering training doesn't provide.

Prompt engineering represents a fundamental shift in how humans interact with computer systems. Instead of learning programming languages to instruct machines, prompt engineers use sophisticated natural language techniques to guide AI behavior. As Andrej Karpathy, Tesla's former chief AI scientist, observed: "The hottest new programming language is English."[42]

The field has exploded in popularity and compensation. Companies are offering six-figure salaries for prompt engineering roles that require humanities backgrounds rather than traditional computer science degrees. The work involves understanding how large language models (LLMs) interpret instructions, testing different approaches to achieve desired outputs, and refining prompts to optimize AI performance.[43]

But prompt engineering represents something deeper than just a new job category—it's evidence of how AI agents are creating entirely new forms of work that exist solely to manage the relationship between humans and artificial intelligence. These jobs wouldn't exist without AI, and they exist specifically because AI systems have become sophisticated enough to require specialized human handlers.

The emergence of prompt engineering also reveals the limits of AI autonomy. Despite promises of fully automated systems, companies are discovering that they need humans who can effectively guide AI behavior, interpret AI outputs, and bridge the gap between what artificial agents can do and what businesses actually need.

LinkedIn shows over 1,000 active prompt engineering job listings in the United States, with roles ranging from $43 to $105 per hour for contract work and full-time salaries reaching into the low six figures.[44] Companies like OpenAI, Google, and Microsoft are hiring prompt engineers not just to improve their AI systems, but to teach other employees how to work effectively with artificial agents.

The field is rapidly professionalizing, with specialized training programs, industry conferences, and emerging best practices. Universities are beginning to offer courses in prompt engineering, and professional organizations are developing certification programs for practitioners.

Yet the long-term viability of prompt engineering as a career remains uncertain. As AI systems become more sophisticated, they may require less human guidance to produce desired outputs. Some experts predict that prompt engineering will evolve into broader "AI interaction design" roles, while others believe the field may become automated as AI systems learn to optimize their own prompts.

What's certain is that prompt engineering represents the first wave of jobs created specifically to manage AI agents—and it won't be the last.

The Customer Service Revolution

While prompt engineers were learning to communicate with AI systems, another workforce transformation was quietly unfolding in call centers and customer service departments across the globe. Companies discovered that AI agents could handle increasingly complex customer interactions, leading to the elimination of thousands of human customer service jobs while creating new hybrid roles that required workers to collaborate with artificial agents in unprecedented ways.

The transformation began subtly at major companies like Bank of America, which deployed an AI assistant called "Erica" to handle routine customer inquiries about account balances, transaction history, and basic banking questions. Initially, Erica operated alongside human customer service representatives, handling simple queries while routing complex issues to human agents.

But the AI agent's capabilities expanded rapidly. By mid-2023, Erica had surpassed 1.5 billion client interactions—and by 2024, that number exceeded 2 billion, with the AI processing approximately 2 million customer interactions daily. The virtual assistant had learned to handle increasingly sophisticated requests, from helping customers monitor recurring subscriptions to providing personalized insights about spending patterns and account history. According to Bank of America, more than 98 percent of users found the information they needed through Erica, "significantly decreasing call center volume and allowing financial specialists to spend time focusing on more complex financial conversations with clients."[45]

The most dramatic example of AI displacement came from Klarna, the Swedish fintech company. In February 2024, CEO Sebastian Siemiatkowski announced that the company's OpenAI-powered chatbot was "doing the equivalent work of 700 full-time agents." Within its first month of operation, the AI assistant had handled 2.3 million conversations—about two-thirds of all customer service chats—across 23 markets and 35 languages.[46] The company claimed customer satisfaction scores matched those of human agents, while resolution times dropped from an average of 11 minutes to under two minutes.

But Klarna's aggressive AI strategy would later prove cautionary. By early 2025, Siemiatkowski publicly admitted the company had "gone too far." The AI-driven transition had negatively affected service quality, with customers reporting frustration over robotic responses and inadequate problem resolution. "From a brand perspective, a company perspective, I just think it's so critical that you are clear to your customer that there will always be a human if you want," Siemiatkowski told Bloomberg as the company began rehiring human staff.[47]

The remaining human customer service workers across industries found their jobs fundamentally changed. Industry observers noted what might be called "emotional labor intensification"—where human workers became responsible primarily for the most stressful aspects of customer service while AI agents handled routine, satisfying interactions that once provided balance and variety. Research on call center work consistently identifies emotional labor as a primary driver of the industry's notoriously high turnover rates, which in some cases climbed above 60 percent annually.[48]

Human agents became a last resort rather than a first contact, handling only the most difficult situations after AI escalation—often encountering customers already frustrated by failed automated interactions. The relationship-building opportunities that once made customer service rewarding diminished as workers spent shifts dealing exclusively with angry customers whose problems were too complex or sensitive for AI resolution.

The AI systems' influence extended beyond individual interactions to reshape the entire structure of customer service work. As IBM and other technology providers explained, these systems used machine learning to "learn from past customer interactions and improve over time without manual updates." Every conversation became training data. AI systems analyzed which types of problems human representatives handled most efficiently and used this information to continuously refine their own capabilities, gradually expanding the scope of problems they could handle independently.

Similar transformations occurred across industries. Insurance companies deployed AI agents to process claims and explain coverage options. Telecommunications companies used artificial assistants to troubleshoot technical problems. Banking industry analysts projected that AI could displace over half of banking jobs in coming years—a prediction Citibank publicly endorsed. The Bureau of Labor Statistics projected a 5 percent decline in customer service representative employment between 2023 and 2033, with approximately 148,800 fewer positions expected due largely to automation.[49]

The workers who remained found themselves trained not in product knowledge and communication skills, but in how to work effectively with AI systems—learning to interpret algorithmic recommendations, override automated decisions when necessary, and handle the emotional aftermath of failed AI interactions. These "AI-augmented" customer service roles required new skills that bridged human empathy and technological literacy. Workers needed to understand how AI systems made decisions so they could explain algorithmic reasoning to confused customers, while also providing the emotional intelligence that artificial agents lacked.

The Hidden Workforce Behind AI

Let's now think about the other side of the AI related labor coin—data labelers and content moderators whose low-paid labor makes these AI tools functional. These workers, primarily located in countries like Kenya, the Philippines, and Venezuela, perform the essential but invisible work of training AI systems to recognize patterns, understand context, and avoid generating harmful content.[50]

The story of this hidden workforce came into sharp focus through the experiences of workers at Sama, a Kenyan outsourcing company contracted by OpenAI to help develop ChatGPT's content-filtering systems. Starting in November 2021, Sama workers began receiving tens of thousands of text samples containing graphic descriptions of violence, sexual abuse, and hate speech. Their job was to read through this disturbing content and label it so that OpenAI's AI systems could learn to recognize and filter similar material in the future.[51]

The work was psychologically devastating. Junior data labelers, who comprised the majority of workers on the OpenAI contract, were paid just $1.32 to $1.44 per hour after taxes to review content that included detailed descriptions of sexual violence, child abuse, and graphic murders. Senior labelers could earn up to $2 per hour if they met all their performance targets.[52]

One Sama worker described being traumatized by reading a graphic description of bestiality involving a child. "That was torture," he said. "You will read a number of statements like that all through the week. By the time it gets to Friday, you are disturbed from thinking through that picture."[53]

Another worker read an erotica scene depicting sexual violence and became confused about how to categorize it, eventually asking OpenAI's researchers for guidance on how to label ambiguous content. These workers were making complex judgments about context, intent, and harm—the kind of nuanced analysis that AI systems couldn't perform independently.[54]

Ephantus Kanyugi was among them. The 30-year-old, who has worked on image labeling since 2018, found work with Remotasks, a subsidiary of Scale AI that provides data labeling services for companies developing autonomous vehicles, medical AI, and computer vision systems. As vice-president of the Data Labelers Association, an 800-strong labor group based in Nairobi, Kanyugi has become a leading voice documenting the exploitation of Kenyan data workers.[55]

Workers like Kanyugi spent their days labeling objects in images and videos—identifying pedestrians, cars, traffic signs, and obstacles that self-driving car algorithms needed to recognize.[56] For each task, workers earned as little as one or two cents, though some more complex tasks paid slightly more. According to multiple investigations, Kenyan workers earned approximately $2 per hour compared to $20 or more for equivalent work in the United States.

The working conditions were harsh. Remotasks used algorithmic monitoring to track worker performance, with payment tied to speed and accuracy. One Kenyan annotator told Privacy International that he had "gotten in the habit of waking up every few hours at night to check his queue for tasks because many jobs pop up, without warning, late at night."[57]

Workers reported being suddenly cut off from payment. "When it gets to the day before payday, they close the account and say that you violated a policy," Kanyugi told CBS News's *60 Minutes*. "There's no recourse or even a way to complain."

The psychological toll of data labeling work varies by project type, but it's consistently severe. Content moderators like those working on social media platforms face the most traumatic material, but even seemingly benign tasks create mental health challenges. Workers report developing anxiety disorders from constant algorithmic monitoring, depression from social isolation, and physical ailments from long hours staring at screens while meeting productivity quotas.[58]

The scale of this hidden workforce is enormous. According to Privacy International, the global data labeling industry relies on millions of "microworkers" who perform small tasks for companies like Scale AI, whose subsidiary Remotasks assigns workers to label everything from photographs to hour-long videos for autonomous vehicle systems.[59] These platforms operate as "humans-as-a-service" marketplaces where employers can outsource cognitive labor to on-demand workers without formal employment relationships.

The geographic distribution of this work reflects global economic inequalities. Although United States-based AI researchers and engineers earn six-figure salaries, the workers who actually train their systems earn as little as $1.46 per hour. Companies like OpenAI, Microsoft, and Google contract with firms like Scale AI, Surge AI, and Sama to access cheaper labor markets while maintaining distance from the working conditions and mental health impacts of data labeling work.[60]

The most disturbing aspect of this global AI supply chain is how it systematically exploits economic desperation. Companies actively seek out workers in countries with high unemployment rates, limited labor protections, and weak currencies. They offer wages that seem competitive locally while being far below what equivalent work would command in developed countries.[61]

Remotasks abruptly shut down its Kenyan operations in March 2024, sending thousands of workers a brief email informing them that their services were no longer needed. Many workers lost weeks of unpaid wages and had no recourse for recovering their earnings. Kwamura was among those left without income or explanation after spending months training AI systems for American companies.[62]

The exploitation became so severe that in May 2024, 97 Kenyan data labelers, content moderators, and AI workers wrote an open letter to President Biden describing their working conditions as "modern-day slavery." The letter detailed how American tech companies systematically abuse African workers, undermine local labor laws, and violate international labor standards.[63]

The workers' experiences highlight a fundamental contradiction in the AI industry's narrative about artificial intelligence. While companies promote AI as advanced technology that can operate autonomously, the reality is that these systems depend entirely on massive amounts of human labor—labor that's often hidden, poorly compensated, and psychologically harmful.

Content moderation work is particularly damaging because it requires workers to spend hours daily viewing the most disturbing content on the Internet. Facebook content moderators in Kenya reported working 18-20 hour shifts, processing 700-1,000 cases with just 7-12 seconds per decision. Many developed severe PTSD from constant exposure to traumatic material.[64]

The mental health impacts are severe and largely unaddressed. Research by the human rights organization Equidem documented over 60 cases of serious mental health harm among 113 data labelers across Kenya, Ghana, Colombia, and the Philippines. Companies provide minimal mental health support despite knowing that the work causes psychological trauma.[65]

In response to these conditions, Kenyan workers formed the Data Labelers Association to advocate for better working conditions, mental health support, and fair compensation. The organization represents a growing movement of AI workers organizing across national boundaries to challenge the exploitative structure of the global AI supply chain.[66]

The tragedy of labor exploitation took a dark turn in March 2025 when Ladi Anzaki Olubunmi, a Nigerian content moderator working in Nairobi, was found dead in her apartment. Although the circumstances remain unclear, her death sparked outrage from labor advocates and renewed calls for systemic reform of AI labor practices.[67]

The Economic Architecture of Agent Nation

The stories of D.K.'s discriminatory hiring experience, Amazon's surveillance systems, Uber's wage algorithms, AI management in healthcare, the rise of prompt engineering, the transformation of customer service, and the exploitation of data labelers represent different facets of a fundamental transformation in how work operates in the digital economy. These aren't isolated incidents or temporary disruptions—they're evidence of a new economic architecture where AI agents increasingly mediate the relationship between workers and employers.

This transformation operates through what I call "algorithmic intermediation"—the insertion of artificial agents between human workers and the economic opportunities they depend on. Instead of workers negotiating directly with employers or competing in transparent labor markets, they now must prove their worth to AI systems that operate according to logic they can't understand or challenge.

The power dynamics of this new system are fundamentally different from traditional employment relationships. When a human supervisor makes a decision about hiring, promotion, or discipline, that decision exists within established frameworks of workplace law, union protection, and social accountability. Workers can appeal decisions, organize collectively, and challenge unfair treatment through recognized legal and social mechanisms.

But when an AI agent makes the same decision, these traditional protections largely disappear. Workers can't negotiate with an algorithm, and they can't appeal to an artificial agent's sense of fairness or empathy. The decision-making process is often opaque, making it impossible to identify bias or challenge discriminatory outcomes.

This shift creates what labor researchers call "algorithmic management"—a system where AI agents exercise direct authority over human workers. Unlike traditional management, which operates through human relationships and social accountability, algorithmic management functions through automated surveillance, evaluation, and discipline that operates beyond the reach of traditional worker protections.[68]

The economic implications extend far beyond individual workplace experiences. When AI agents systematically discriminate against certain groups in hiring, the effects compound across entire communities and industries. When algorithmic wage systems exploit worker desperation, they create downward pressure on compensation across entire sectors. When surveillance systems monitor workers' every movement, they normalize a level of workplace control that would be considered authoritarian if implemented by human managers.

These changes are happening at unprecedented speed and scale. Unlike previous technological disruptions that unfolded over decades, AI agents are being deployed across multiple industries simultaneously, creating rapid changes in working conditions that outpace workers' ability to adapt or organize effective responses.

The geographic distribution of AI work also creates new forms of global inequality. Although highly paid prompt engineers work for Silicon Valley companies, the data labelers who train AI systems earn subsistence wages in countries with weak labor protections. This global division of AI labor reinforces existing patterns of economic exploitation while creating new forms of technological dependence.

Perhaps most troubling is how AI agents are creating new forms of work precarity that transcend traditional employment categories. Gig workers face algorithmic wage discrimination, while traditional employees confront AI surveillance and evaluation systems. Even highly skilled professionals like nurses and customer service representatives find their expertise being systematically captured by AI systems that gradually reduce the human contribution to their work.

There's a whole spectrum of possibilities of AI-induced labor here. On one end of the spectrum, workers are helping build better AI systems by labeling, filtering, and prompt engineering. On the other end of the spectrum, workers are being governed by an AI system making decisions about their hiring, wages, and terminations. We are working for these agents and also being worked on by them. The result is what economists call "algorithmic proletarianization"—the gradual reduction of human workers to sources of data and training examples for AI systems that will eventually replace them. Workers aren't just losing jobs to automation; they're being forced to train their own replacements while experiencing degraded working conditions and reduced autonomy.

The Resistance Begins

Despite the challenges posed by algorithmic management, workers are beginning to organize new forms of resistance adapted to the realities of AI-mediated work. The formation of Kenya's Data Labelers Association, the ACLU's lawsuit on behalf of D.K., the union organizing efforts at Amazon's warehouses, and the nursing union restrictions on AI scheduling systems represent early attempts to establish worker power in the age of artificial agents.

These organizing efforts face unique challenges that traditional labor movements didn't encounter. How do you organize workers who are scattered across multiple countries and platforms? How do you negotiate with companies that claim their AI decisions are objective and unbiased? How do you challenge algorithmic discrimination when the decision-making process is hidden behind proprietary code?

The answers are still emerging, but certain patterns are becoming clear. Successful organizing in the AI economy requires international coordination, technical expertise, and new forms of legal strategy that can address algorithmic bias and automated discrimination. Workers need data scientists who can audit AI systems, lawyers who understand algorithmic decision-making, and organizers who can build solidarity across geographic and technological boundaries.

The most effective challenges to algorithmic management have combined worker organizing with technical analysis and legal intervention. The ACLU's case against HireVue, for example, draws on research demonstrating how the company's AI system discriminates against deaf and minority candidates. Privacy International's complaint against Amazon's surveillance systems combines worker testimony with technical analysis of the company's monitoring infrastructure.

Across the healthcare sector, nurses have begun pushing back against algorithmic systems that override their clinical judgment. National Nurses United, the largest nursing union in the United States representing over

225,000 members, has developed a "Nurses and Patients' Bill of Rights" outlining principles for AI use in healthcare settings. The document demands that nurses retain the right to exercise professional judgment and override AI-generated recommendations without threat of discipline.[69]

These principles have translated into concrete contract victories. At Northwell South Shore University Hospital in New York, nurses secured provisions requiring union review of artificial intelligence technology before implementation—a first for nurses' union contracts in the state.[70] At Keck Medicine of USC, nurses on the professional practice committee successfully bargained for language ensuring that only a licensed registered nurse can make final decisions about patient acuity and nursing care hours, pushing back against the Clairvia scheduling algorithm. "We demanded to bargain," explained one nurse board member. "We wanted a commitment from the hospital, in writing, that you are going to leave responsibility for patient classification and acuity up to the bedside nurse."[71]

Beyond healthcare, workers displaced by automation have increasingly turned to collective bargaining as a tool for shaping how AI enters their workplaces. In 2023, the Las Vegas Culinary Workers Union negotiated a groundbreaking agreement with major casinos requiring advance notice and the opportunity to bargain over AI implementation. The contract also guarantees severance pay, continued benefits, and recall rights for workers displaced by automation. That same year, the Writers Guild of America and SAG-AFTRA conducted historic strikes that resulted in landmark agreements restricting how studios can use generative AI—demonstrating that collective action can establish guardrails around technology deployment even in industries where AI threatens fundamental aspects of workers' livelihoods.[72]

The global nature of AI work has also sparked new forms of international solidarity. In May 2023, over 150 content moderators gathered in Nairobi and voted to establish the African Content Moderators Union—the first such union on the continent. These workers, employed by outsourcing companies like Sama and Majorel to moderate content for Facebook, TikTok, and ChatGPT, had endured traumatic working conditions reviewing graphic content depicting violence, child abuse, and hate speech, often for wages as low as $1.50 per hour. "For too long we, the workers powering the AI revolution, were treated as different and less than moderators," said Richard Mathenge, a former ChatGPT content moderator who helped organize the union. "Our work is just as important and it is also dangerous."[73]

The union's formation built on earlier organizing efforts that had been suppressed. In 2019, moderator Daniel Motaung and over 100 colleagues at Facebook's Nairobi hub attempted to form a group called the Alliance to negotiate over pay and mental healthcare. The effort was crushed, and Motaung was fired and forced to leave Kenya. But investigative reporting in 2022 lifted the lid on the exploitation, triggering a wave of legal action that planted the seeds for the union's eventual creation.[74] The movement has since grown to approximately 400 members from Kenya, Nigeria, Ghana, Uganda, Ethiopia, and South Africa.

According to Martha Dark, co-founder of Foxglove, the UK-based legal nonprofit supporting the moderators' legal challenges, the industry's exploitative conditions have spawned cross-border organizing efforts. "There are content moderators that are coming together from Poland, America, Kenya, and Germany talking about what the challenges are that they experience when trying to organize in the context of working for Big Tech companies like Facebook and TikTok," she explained.[75] These partnerships are still nascent, but they represent an emerging recognition that the algorithmic systems shaping workers' lives operate across borders—and that resistance must do the same.

These efforts are creating new forms of worker power that specifically address the challenges of AI-mediated work. Instead of simply demanding better wages or working conditions, workers are fighting for algorithmic transparency, bias auditing, and human oversight of AI decision-making systems.

The stakes of these struggles extend far beyond the immediate interests of individual workers or industries. The patterns of algorithmic management being established today will shape the future of work for decades to come. If AI agents are allowed to operate without meaningful oversight or accountability, they will create new forms of workplace authoritarianism that could undermine the basic principles of worker rights and democratic governance.

The Future of Human-AI Collaboration

The emergence of Agent Nation doesn't necessarily mean the end of meaningful work or human agency. But it does require fundamentally rethinking how we organize economic relationships in an era where artificial agents play an increasingly active role in managing human labor.

The prompt engineering phenomenon suggests one possible future: the creation of entirely new categories of work that emerge from human-AI collaboration rather than competition. These jobs require uniquely human skills—creativity, empathy, cultural understanding—while leveraging AI capabilities for scale and efficiency.

Similarly, the evolution of customer service work, while eliminating many traditional jobs, has also created opportunities for workers who can effectively bridge human and artificial intelligence. These "AI-augmented" roles require new skills that combine emotional intelligence with technical literacy, suggesting pathways for human workers to remain relevant in an increasingly automated economy.

But realizing this potential requires addressing the current patterns of exploitation and discrimination that characterize much AI-mediated work. Companies must be held accountable for the bias embedded in their AI systems. Workers need legal protections against algorithmic discrimination. The hidden workforce of data labelers and content moderators deserves fair compensation and mental health support.

Most fundamentally, we need new frameworks for democratic governance of AI agents that operate in workplace settings. Just as we developed labor laws to govern human managers, we need algorithmic accountability standards that ensure AI agents operate according to principles of fairness, transparency, and human dignity.

The healthcare example demonstrates both the risks and opportunities of AI in professional settings. When implemented without worker input, AI scheduling systems can create exploitative working conditions that harm both employees and patients. But when workers have a voice in AI deployment decisions, these same technologies can potentially improve working conditions by reducing administrative burdens and optimizing resource allocation.

The key difference lies in who controls the AI agents and for what purposes they're deployed. AI systems designed primarily to reduce labor costs and maximize productivity will inevitably conflict with worker interests. But AI agents designed to enhance human capabilities and improve working conditions could become powerful tools for worker empowerment.

This requires moving beyond the current paradigm where AI development is driven primarily by capital efficiency toward approaches that prioritize human flourishing and democratic participation. Workers must have meaningful input into the design and deployment of AI systems that affect their jobs, and they need legal protections that ensure artificial agents operate fairly and transparently.

The stories explored in this chapter—from D.K.'s fight against discriminatory hiring algorithms to the Kenyan data labelers organizing for better working conditions—represent the early stages of a broader struggle over how AI agents will be integrated into the economy. The outcome of this struggle will determine whether artificial agents become tools that enhance human capability and create new opportunities, or weapons that automate exploitation and undermine worker power.

The choice is still ours to make, but time is running short. Every day, more companies deploy AI agents to manage workers, evaluate candidates, and determine compensation. Each deployment creates precedents that become harder to challenge as they become normalized. The window for shaping how Agent Nation evolves is closing, but it hasn't closed yet.

The workers fighting back like Kenya's Data Labelers Association—aren't asking to eliminate AI from the workplace. They're demanding that artificial agents operate according to principles of fairness, transparency, and human dignity. Their struggle will determine whether we build an AI economy that serves human flourishing or one that treats humans as disposable inputs in an algorithmic optimization process.

CHAPTER 3

Algorithmic Governance

Loomis v. Wisconsin began as a routine sentencing hearing in a La Crosse County courtroom, but it would become one of the most significant challenges to algorithmic governance in American legal history. On February 14, 2013, Eric Loomis pled guilty to attempting to flee an officer and operating a vehicle without the owner's consent. What happened next revealed how artificial agents had quietly inserted themselves into the most sacred processes of democratic justice.[1]

During Loomis's sentencing hearing, Judge Scott Horne consulted more than just the facts of the case, the defendant's criminal history, and the prosecutor's recommendations. He also relied on a risk assessment generated by COMPAS—Correctional Offender Management Profiling for Alternative Sanctions—an AI system that analyzed over 130 factors to predict Loomis's likelihood of reoffending.[2]

The algorithm's verdict was harsh: COMPAS rated Loomis as "high risk" for both general recidivism and violent recidivism. The artificial agent had processed his criminal history, demographics, and responses to a psychological questionnaire through proprietary machine learning models to generate these scores. Judge Horne, influenced by the algorithmic assessment, sentenced Loomis to six years in prison and five years of extended supervision—a punishment that exceeded what prosecutors had requested.[3]

C. Shah, *Agent Nation*, https://doi.org/10.1007/979-8-8688-2454-8_3

But there was a problem that wouldn't become apparent until Loomis appealed his sentence: neither he nor his attorney could understand how COMPAS had reached its conclusions. The algorithm's decision-making process was protected as a trade secret by its manufacturer, Northpointe Inc. The artificial agent that had influenced Loomis's fate operated as a black box, making consequential judgments about human freedom while hiding its reasoning behind proprietary code.[4]

Loomis's case eventually reached the Wisconsin Supreme Court, where it became a landmark confrontation between traditional principles of due process and the new reality of algorithmic governance. How could a defendant meaningfully challenge a sentence if the AI system that influenced it couldn't be examined? How could judges ensure fairness if they couldn't understand the logic underlying algorithmic recommendations?

The court's 2016 decision revealed the profound challenges that AI agents pose to democratic institutions. While the justices acknowledged serious concerns about COMPAS's opacity and potential bias, they upheld Loomis's sentence, reasoning that judges could continue using algorithmic risk assessments as long as they didn't rely on them exclusively.[5] The ruling established a precedent that would shape how thousands of criminal defendants across America would be sentenced in the years to come.

By 2024, COMPAS and similar AI systems were being used in sentencing decisions in all 50 states, processing over 1 million criminal cases annually.[6] These artificial agents had become embedded in the machinery of American justice, making predictions about human behavior that influenced everything from bail decisions to parole hearings to prison sentences.

But Loomis's story was just the beginning of a much larger transformation. Across America, AI agents were quietly assuming roles that had traditionally belonged to human civic institutions—from determining which neighborhoods received police attention to deciding which families qualified for social services. The algorithmic governance revolution was reshaping democracy itself, often without the knowledge or consent of the citizens it affected.

The Rise of Predictive Policing

Although COMPAS was learning to assess individual defendants, another generation of algorithmic systems was making broader decisions about public safety across entire cities. The Chicago Police Department's Strategic Subject List, launched in 2012, represents one of the most controversial experiments in predictive policing ever attempted. The system deployed algorithms to identify specific individuals likely to be involved in gun violence—either as perpetrators or victims—and flag them for police intervention.[7]

The algorithm, developed by the Illinois Institute of Technology and funded through a Department of Justice grant, calculated risk scores based on eight factors: the number of times an individual had been a shooting victim, age at most recent arrest, number of times victimized by aggravated battery or assault, prior arrests for violent offenses, gang affiliation, prior narcotics arrests, trends in recent criminal activity, and prior arrests for unlawful weapon use. Notably, race and gender were not explicitly included as variables, though critics argued the inputs served as proxies for both.[8]

The scope of the program was staggering. By July 2018, nearly 400,000 people had been assigned risk scores by the algorithm—essentially every person arrested by the Chicago Police Department over a six-year period. Individuals received scores ranging from 0 to 500, with those scoring above 250 subject to heightened police scrutiny. Analysis by the nonprofit Upturn revealed that more than two-thirds of everyone in the database—over 287,000 people—exceeded this threshold.[9]

The most troubling aspect of Chicago's system was how it threatened to perpetuate existing patterns of discriminatory enforcement. A 2017

Chicago Sun-Times investigation found that 85 percent of those with the highest risk scores were African American. The algorithm learned from historical arrest data that reflected decades of racially disparate policing practices, then used those patterns to guide future police attention. Areas and individuals who had been heavily policed in the past received even more scrutiny from the algorithmic system, creating feedback loops that risked intensifying racial disparities in police contact.[10]

Robert McDaniel experienced this algorithmic targeting firsthand when Chicago police arrived at his home in the Austin neighborhood in August 2013. Commander Barbara West informed him that the department's computer system had identified him as likely to be involved in gun violence. McDaniel, then 22 years old, had been arrested multiple times on suspicion of minor offenses but had only one misdemeanor conviction—no violent criminal history, no gun violations. Yet the algorithm had analyzed his social connections, including a close friend who had been killed, and concluded he was at elevated risk.[11]

"I haven't done nothing that the next kid growing up hadn't done," McDaniel told the *Chicago Tribune* after the visit. He was offended at being singled out by police and nervous that neighbors who witnessed the visit might suspect him of being a police informant.[12]

The police visit proved consequential in ways the algorithm's designers likely never anticipated. According to reporting by Matt Stroud in *The Verge,* McDaniel's inclusion on the heat list made him a target of suspicion in his own community. A day or two after being filmed by documentary makers exploring the program, McDaniel received a call from an acquaintance who wanted him to explain why police had visited his home and why he was being documented. As he walked to meet them, a car pulled up and a man inside fired multiple shots. One bullet struck McDaniel in the knee. Years later, in August 2020, he was shot again in an alleyway near his home. In McDaniel's view, the heat list caused the very harm it was designed to prevent—a grim self-fulfilling prophecy.[13]

Research by the RAND Corporation found that an early version of Chicago's program "does not appear to have been successful in reducing gun violence." The study concluded that individuals on the Strategic Subject List were not more or less likely to become victims of homicide or shooting than a comparison group—meaning the algorithm failed at its core predictive function. Chicago police officials contested the findings, claiming the version RAND evaluated had since been significantly updated.[14]

Perhaps most concerning, Chicago's police department struggled to explain how its system reached conclusions about specific individuals. The algorithms processed multiple variables through models that produced risk scores without fully revealing their underlying logic. When civil liberties advocates and journalists pressed for details about how the system worked, officials initially withheld information, claiming operational sensitivity. Only after the *Chicago Sun-Times* filed a lawsuit did the department release a de-identified version of the database in 2017.[15]

"This is basically government decision-making turned over to an algorithm without any transparency about it," said Karen Sheley, director of the ACLU of Illinois' Police Practices Project. The opacity of the system made it nearly impossible for individuals to understand why they had been flagged, let alone challenge their inclusion.[16]

In November 2019, the Chicago Police Department quietly discontinued the Strategic Subject List. A report by the city's Office of Inspector General identified multiple areas of concern, including "the unreliability of risk scores and tiers," "improperly trained sworn personnel," and "a lack of controls for internal and external access." The department acknowledged what critics had long argued: the data-scraping effort had not reduced violence. The reversal followed a similar decision by the Los Angeles Police Department to abandon its own predictive policing list the previous year.[17]

Chicago's experience with predictive policing reflects a broader pattern occurring in law enforcement agencies across the United States.

Cities from Los Angeles to New York have experimented with algorithmic systems to analyze crime patterns and direct police resources. These systems promised to make policing more efficient and objective, but Chicago's failed experiment demonstrates how algorithmic authority can operate outside traditional frameworks of accountability—creating new risks even as it claims to reduce old ones.[18]

The artificial agents powering predictive policing systems don't just analyze data—they make autonomous decisions about which communities receive police attention and which individuals are treated as potential threats. These AI systems have become invisible partners in law enforcement, shaping police behavior and citizen experiences while operating beyond public scrutiny or democratic oversight.

Municipal Algorithms in Action

While predictive policing systems were learning to direct law enforcement resources, AI agents were simultaneously assuming control over basic municipal services that citizens depend on daily. New York City's Automated Decision Systems Task Force, established by Local Law 49 of 2018 and formally convened by Mayor Bill de Blasio in May 2018, was tasked with identifying and evaluating the algorithmic systems that had quietly embedded themselves in city government.[19]

What the task force and subsequent investigations discovered was remarkable: AI agents were making autonomous decisions about everything from school admissions and public housing placements to building inspections and child welfare prioritization. By 2024, at least 46 algorithmic tools were officially reported across city agencies under Local Law 35 of 2022, with the Department of Health and Mental Hygiene and the Administration for Children's Services among the heaviest users.[20]

Mary Louis experienced algorithmic governance firsthand when she applied for an apartment in Massachusetts in the spring of 2021. Louis, a Black woman who had paid her rent on time for 16 years, was excited about moving into a new home. Instead of meeting with human decision-makers who could consider her specific circumstances, Louis's application was processed by SafeRent Solutions, a tenant screening company that uses algorithms to generate "SafeRent Scores" for landlords nationwide.[21]

The algorithm's decision was swift but devastating: Louis received an email from the management company stating her application had been denied. When she tried to understand the reasoning behind this determination, the response was blunt: "We do not accept appeals and cannot override the outcome of the Tenant Screening."[22]

Louis's situation was particularly frustrating because she held a housing voucher that covered approximately 69 percent of her monthly rent—a federal benefit designed to ensure housing stability for low-income families. But SafeRent's algorithm did not factor in the value of her voucher. Instead, the system placed heavy weight on credit history and non-tenancy debts, factors that systematically disadvantaged Black and Hispanic applicants who, due to historical inequities, often have lower median credit scores than white applicants.[23]

"Everything is based on numbers. You don't get the individual empathy from them," Louis later said. "There is no beating the system. The system is always going to beat us." Louis became the lead plaintiff in a class action lawsuit alleging that SafeRent's algorithm violated the Fair Housing Act by systematically discriminating against Black and Hispanic applicants and housing voucher holders. In January 2023, the U.S. Department of Justice and the Department of Housing and Urban Development filed a Statement of Interest in the case, explaining how the Fair Housing Act applies to algorithm-based tenant screening systems.[24]

In November 2024, a federal judge approved a settlement in the case, with SafeRent agreeing to pay over $2.2 million and roll back certain parts of its screening products that the lawsuit alleged were discriminatory. Under the settlement, SafeRent can no longer include its score feature on tenant screening reports for applicants using housing vouchers.[25] But the case revealed how artificial agents in housing can perpetuate systemic inequalities while hiding their reasoning behind technical complexity.

New York's automated decision systems extend far beyond housing allocation. The Administration for Children's Services uses an AI tool called the Severe Harm Predictive Model to evaluate reports of child abuse and neglect, automatically prioritizing cases based on algorithmic risk scores. Launched in 2018 and developed by an internal data team at the agency, the system uses 279 variables to score families for risk, based on cases from 2013 and 2014 that ended in a child being severely harmed.[26]

Karlena Hamblin, a Black mother from Brownsville, Brooklyn, has experienced this algorithmic surveillance firsthand. ACS had been watching her and her family since she was three months pregnant, when the agency held a pre-birth conference to discuss her family's future. "The baby's not even here yet and you're already talking about removing her?" Hamblin recalled asking. The algorithm factors in variables that are largely outside a caretaker's control and align closely with socioeconomic status: the neighborhood a family lives in, the mother's age, the number of siblings a child has, and even a caretaker's mental health history.[27]

The racial implications are stark. In New York City, Black families are reported to ACS at seven times the rate of white families and are 13 times more likely to have a child removed. Roughly 90 percent of the families ACS investigates are Black or Brown.[28] While the algorithm does not explicitly use race, it relies on neighborhood, socioeconomic factors, and prior agency contact—variables that critics argue serve as proxies for race and poverty. "My neighborhood alone makes me more likely to be abusive or neglectful?" Hamblin asked. "That's because we look at poverty as neglect and the neighborhoods they identify have very low resources."

The cumulative effect of these municipal AI systems is the creation of what scholar John Cheney-Lippold first termed "algorithmic identity"—and what researchers have since expanded into the concept of "algorithmic citizenship."[29] In this framework, citizens' access to government services and protection is mediated by artificial agents that operate according to criteria they cannot understand or challenge. Instead of interacting with human representatives who can exercise judgment and respond to individual circumstances, New Yorkers increasingly encounter AI systems that make decisions based on pattern recognition and statistical correlation.

This transformation poses fundamental challenges to democratic governance. Traditional municipal services operated through human relationships, professional judgment, and bureaucratic accountability mechanisms that citizens could navigate and challenge. But algorithmic governance creates new forms of administrative power that operate at machine speed and scale while remaining largely invisible to the people they affect.

The New York City Automated Decision Systems Task Force ultimately recommended greater transparency and accountability for municipal AI systems, but implementation was slow and incomplete. Task Force member Albert Fox Cahn, Executive Director of the Surveillance Technology Oversight Project, described the process as a "spectacular failure," noting that city officials had hoped for a task force report that was more of a rubber stamp than what reformers had in mind. The task force was never even provided with a comprehensive list of city-operated algorithmic systems.[30]

The Child Welfare Algorithm

Perhaps nowhere is the tension between algorithmic efficiency and human judgment starker than in child welfare systems, where AI agents are making some of the most consequential decisions in government: whether to separate children from their families. Allegheny County, Pennsylvania, which includes Pittsburgh, became a national testing ground for this transformation when it deployed the Allegheny Family Screening Tool (AFST) in August 2016.[31]

The AFST system analyzes hundreds of variables from county databases to generate risk scores for families reported to child protective services. The algorithm draws on data from the county's integrated data warehouse, including child welfare records, criminal justice involvement, mental health treatment records, public benefits usage, and birth records. Based on this analysis, the system generates a score from 1 to 20 that predicts the probability a child will be removed from their home and placed in foster care within two years of being referred to the agency.[32]

The system's approach to risk assessment reflects broader problems with how algorithmic tools learn from biased historical data. Political scientist Virginia Eubanks spent a year reporting on the AFST for her influential book *Automating Inequality*, documenting how the algorithm systematically disadvantages families who have sought help from county agencies. In an interview with Erin Dalton, Director of Allegheny County's Office of Data Analysis, Research, and Evaluation, Dalton acknowledged the system's limitations: "We definitely oversample the poor. All of the data systems we have are biased. We still think this data can be helpful in protecting kids."[33]

Eubanks found that the AFST creates what she calls a "digital poorhouse"—a system that confuses "parenting-while-poor with poor parenting" because it only has access to data about families that have received public resources. Families who can afford private mental health counseling, for instance, leave no trace in the county's databases, while those who seek help through public programs accumulate data points that the algorithm interprets as risk factors. The system essentially punishes families for reaching out for support, interpreting their requests for assistance as indicators of dysfunction rather than responsible help-seeking behavior.[34]

The concerns raised by families and advocates eventually attracted federal attention. In 2022 and 2023, the Associated Press conducted an extensive investigation into the AFST, revealing potential bias and transparency issues. Following the AP's reporting, several civil rights complaints were filed with the Justice Department's Civil Rights Division. Attorneys from the Civil Rights Division contacted advocates and researchers, expressing concern that the algorithm could "harden bias against people with disabilities, including families with mental health issues."[35]

Robin Frank, a veteran family law attorney in Pittsburgh, filed a complaint with the Justice Department on behalf of a client with an intellectual disability who was fighting to regain custody of his daughter. "I think it's important for people to be aware of what their rights are," Frank told the Associated Press. "And to the extent that we don't have a lot of information when there seemingly are valid questions about the algorithm, it's important to have some oversight."[36]

The algorithmic bias became even more troubling when independent researchers discovered significant racial disparities in AFST risk scores. A 2023 study by researchers including Katherine Rittenhouse found that the AFST produces racially disproportionate scores. Research published by the ACLU and the Human Rights Data Analysis Group revealed that if the algorithm's recommendations had been followed without human intervention, approximately 71 percent of Black children referred would have been screened in for investigation, compared to substantially lower rates for white children. The algorithm, designed to reduce bias, was instead automating and potentially amplifying historical patterns of discriminatory child welfare practices.[37]

Allegheny County officials have defended the AFST system by arguing that it improves decision-making consistency and that human screeners retain ultimate authority over whether to investigate. The county commissioned independent evaluations by Stanford University and Hornby Zeller Associates, which found that the tool increased accuracy for children screened in for investigation. County officials also note that screeners can and do override the algorithm's recommendations—supervisors overrode about a quarter of mandatory "screen-in" decisions in the system's early years.[38]

But these defenses miss a fundamental problem: even county officials acknowledge that roughly 30 percent of cases classified as highest risk by the AFST are ultimately thrown out as baseless after investigation. This error rate occurs at the most consequential decision point in the system—where a high AFST score can trigger a mandatory investigation that, regardless of its outcome, creates a formal record that follows families permanently.[39]

The opacity of the AFST algorithm creates additional problems for families trying to understand or challenge their risk scores. Nico'Lee Biddle, a former Allegheny County child welfare worker who spent nearly a decade in the system, described the frustration of not being able to explain the algorithm's logic to families: "We could see the report and that decision, but we were never able to see the actual tool." As Biddle noted, "When you have technology designed by humans, the bias is going to show up in the algorithms. If they designed a perfect tool, it really doesn't matter, because it's designed from very imperfect data systems."[40]

The ACLU's 2023 audit of the AFST, conducted with the Human Rights Data Analysis Group, found that algorithmic design choices function as hidden policy decisions with potentially discriminatory effects. The audit revealed that families often don't even know the county is using the AFST, let alone how it functions or how to raise concerns about it. Furthermore, government databases feeding the algorithm are rife with errors, and the tool itself has experienced glitches that produced erroneous scores. These challenges demonstrate what the ACLU called "the urgent need for transparency, independent oversight, and meaningful recourse when algorithms are deployed in high-stakes decision-making contexts like child welfare."[41]

The Allegheny County experience has been replicated in child welfare systems across the United States. Similar algorithmic risk assessment tools have been implemented in Los Angeles County, California, and in counties across Colorado, with jurisdictions nationwide considering adoption. Oregon discontinued its algorithm in 2022 over concerns about racial bias.

These AI agents now influence decisions affecting hundreds of thousands of families annually, often operating with minimal oversight or public awareness.[42]

Algorithmic Redistricting and Democratic Representation

AI agents have moved well beyond hiring and criminal justice—they now govern access to housing, education, and healthcare with the same opacity and the same lack of accountability. Often, those who are deploying or integrating such agentic services do it to help them lessen the burden or fill in a gap created by lack of adequate human labor, but what we see repeatedly is that such deployment usually doesn't stop there. Worse, given how common and acceptable this has become, people have also been using AI agents' decisions to argue that human biases are not involved. But why should we believe that these agents are not biased or that they don't have an agenda?

Following the 2020 census, state legislatures across America began using sophisticated computer mapping tools to redraw electoral boundaries, creating new opportunities for automated gerrymandering that could influence election outcomes for decades to come.[43]

North Carolina's redistricting process following the 2020 census revealed how computer-assisted mapping could be used to manipulate democratic representation. The Republican-controlled state legislature used redistricting software to analyze census demographics, voting history by precinct, and partisan registration patterns to draw district boundaries that maximized electoral advantage.[44]

Dr. Jowei Chen, Associate Professor of Political Science at the University of Michigan, has developed computer simulation techniques to identify gerrymandered maps and has testified as an expert witness in redistricting cases across the country, including in North Carolina,

Pennsylvania, Michigan, and Utah. Chen's methodology involves generating thousands of alternative districting plans that follow traditional, nonpartisan criteria—equalizing population, maximizing geographic compactness, and preserving county and municipal boundaries—then comparing the enacted plan to this baseline to identify statistical outliers.[45]

In North Carolina's 2021 redistricting litigation, Chen testified that he used a computer algorithm to generate 1,000 different ways of drawing the state's 14 congressional districts. His analysis found that only 3 percent of these computer-generated maps produced the 10-4 Republican split that the legislature's map would create. Chen concluded that the enacted plan was "a partisan outlier" whose Republican bias "cannot be explained by North Carolina's political geography."[46]

The Princeton Gerrymandering Project, which conducts nonpartisan analyses of district maps nationwide, gave North Carolina's 2021 congressional map an "F" grade for partisan fairness. The organization found "significant Republican advantage" in all three maps—congressional, state House, and state Senate—that the legislature approved. According to the Princeton analysis, the congressional map would likely lead to electing 10 or 11 Republicans and only 3 or 4 Democrats in a state that is closely divided between the parties.[47]

The maps drew immediate legal challenge. Rebecca Harper and other North Carolina voters filed suit, arguing that the 2021 maps constituted unconstitutional partisan gerrymanders that violated the state constitution's guarantees of free elections, equal protection, and freedom of speech and assembly. In February 2022, the North Carolina Supreme Court agreed, ruling that the congressional and legislative maps were unconstitutional partisan gerrymanders. The court found that the maps were "more carefully crafted to favor Republicans than at least 99.9999 percent" of all possible North Carolina district maps following the legislature's own criteria.[48]

The case subsequently became the vehicle for a major U.S. Supreme Court case, *Moore v. Harper,* in which Republican legislators argued that state courts had no authority to review congressional redistricting for compliance with state constitutions—a radical legal theory known as the "independent state legislature" doctrine. In June 2023, the Supreme Court rejected this theory, affirming that state courts can serve as a check on legislative redistricting abuses.[49]

However, the North Carolina story took another turn. After the 2022 midterm elections shifted the state Supreme Court from a Democratic to Republican majority, the new court agreed to rehear the Harper case. In April 2023, the reconstituted court overruled its previous decision, holding that partisan gerrymandering claims are not justiciable under the North Carolina Constitution. The reversal allowed the Republican-drawn maps to remain in effect.[50]

The use of computer-assisted redistricting has spread rapidly across the United States, with both Republican- and Democratic-controlled legislatures using mapping software to maximize their electoral advantage. As the Princeton Gerrymandering Project has documented, these tools enable mapmakers to analyze voting patterns at granular levels and optimize district boundaries with mathematical precision that far exceeds traditional mapping techniques.[51]

Perhaps most troubling, the redistricting process often occurs with limited transparency. While some states have adopted independent redistricting commissions or required public input, many legislatures conduct mapping behind closed doors, making it difficult for courts or voting rights advocates to understand how district boundaries were manipulated. As one North Carolina voter testified during public comment on the proposed maps: "This is gerrymandering at its worst."[52]

The transformation of redistricting through computer-assisted mapping represents a significant challenge to democratic governance. Instead of creating districts that fairly represent communities, these tools can be used to optimize for partisan advantage while hiding manipulation behind technical complexity. The result is technology being used to undermine the basic principle of representative democracy: that voters should choose their representatives, rather than representatives choosing their voters.[53]

The Accountability Crisis

The stories of COMPAS in criminal sentencing, predictive policing in Chicago, municipal algorithms in New York, child welfare AI in Allegheny County, and algorithmic redistricting in North Carolina reveal a common pattern: AI agents are making increasingly consequential decisions about citizens' lives while operating beyond traditional mechanisms of democratic accountability.

Unlike human government officials who can be questioned, challenged, and held responsible for their decisions, AI agents operate according to logic that often can't be explained or understood. When Eric Loomis asked how COMPAS had evaluated his recidivism risk, he was told the algorithm's reasoning was a trade secret. When Robert McDaniel questioned why Chicago police had identified him as likely to commit gun violence, officers couldn't explain the predictive policing system's logic. When Mary Louis challenged her tenant screening score in federal court, or when Karlena Hamblin sought to understand why New York's child welfare algorithm flagged her family, they encountered systems whose decision-making processes remained largely opaque.[54]

This opacity creates what legal scholars call a "due process deficit" in algorithmic governance. Traditional principles of democratic accountability assume that government decisions can be examined, questioned, and appealed through established legal and political processes. But when AI agents make these decisions through complex machine learning processes that even their creators don't fully understand, these accountability mechanisms break down.[55]

The problem extends beyond individual cases to encompass broader questions of democratic legitimacy. Government derives its authority from the consent of the governed, but how can citizens meaningfully consent to algorithmic governance they can't understand? How can democratic institutions maintain legitimacy when critical decisions are made by artificial agents that operate according to logic their users can't explain?[56]

The scale and speed of algorithmic decision-making further complicate traditional oversight mechanisms. Chicago's predictive policing system processes hundreds of thousands of data points daily to generate risk scores for entire neighborhoods. New York's automated decision systems make thousands of determinations about city services every hour. These AI agents operate at temporal and spatial scales that exceed human capacity for meaningful review or oversight.[57]

Research by the AI Now Institute found that government agencies often lack the technical expertise necessary to oversee the AI systems they deploy. Agency officials frequently can't evaluate whether algorithmic systems are working correctly, producing biased outcomes, or operating according to their stated objectives. This creates a situation where public servants are accountable for decisions made by AI agents they don't understand.[58]

The procurement process for government AI systems further obscures accountability. Agencies typically purchase algorithmic tools from private vendors who claim their systems are proprietary intellectual property that can't be disclosed publicly. This arrangement allows companies to sell AI agents to government while shielding the decision-making logic from scrutiny by citizens, advocates, or oversight bodies.[59]

Perhaps most troubling, many government AI systems lack basic safeguards against discriminatory outcomes. The Algorithmic Accountability Act, proposed in the U.S. Congress multiple times since 2019, would require federal agencies to assess AI systems for bias and discrimination before deployment. But the legislation has never been enacted, leaving government agencies free to implement AI agents without meaningful evaluation of their fairness or accuracy.[60]

Emerging Models of Algorithmic Accountability

Despite these challenges, some jurisdictions are beginning to develop new approaches to governing AI agents in democratic institutions. The European Union's AI Act, which took effect in 2024, represents the most comprehensive attempt to regulate algorithmic systems used by government agencies.[61]

The AI Act classifies government AI systems based on their risk level and imposes corresponding oversight requirements. High-risk applications like criminal risk assessment, child welfare screening, and immigration decision-making must undergo algorithmic impact assessments before deployment and regular auditing afterward. The legislation also grants citizens' rights to understand and challenge algorithmic decisions that affect them.[62]

Amsterdam's Algorithm Register provides another model for algorithmic transparency in government. The city maintains a public database of all AI systems used by municipal agencies, including descriptions of their purpose, data sources, decision-making logic, and potential risks. Citizens can search the register to understand which algorithmic systems might affect them and request additional information about their operation.[63]

Similarly, Helsinki's AI Ethics Committee reviews all proposed AI deployments by city agencies, evaluating their potential impact on citizen rights and democratic values. The committee includes technical experts, ethicists, and community representatives who assess whether algorithmic systems align with the city's democratic governance principles.[64]

In the United States, some cities and states are beginning to adopt algorithmic accountability ordinances that require government agencies to disclose their use of AI systems and assess their impact on different communities. San Francisco's Surveillance Technology Ordinance requires city agencies to obtain public approval before deploying AI systems that could affect citizen privacy or civil liberties.[65]

These emerging accountability frameworks share several common elements: requirements for transparency about AI system deployment, assessments of algorithmic impact on different communities, mechanisms for citizen input on AI governance decisions, and processes for ongoing monitoring and evaluation of algorithmic outcomes.[66]

However, implementing meaningful algorithmic accountability faces significant challenges. Government agencies often lack the technical expertise necessary to evaluate AI systems effectively. Vendors resist transparency requirements that might reveal proprietary algorithms. And the rapid pace of AI development makes it difficult for regulatory frameworks to keep pace with technological change.[67]

The Future of Democratic AI Governance

The transformation of government through AI agents represents both an opportunity and a threat to democratic institutions. On one hand, algorithmic systems can potentially make government more efficient, consistent, and responsive to citizen needs. AI agents can process information at scales that exceed human capacity, identify patterns that human officials might miss, and operate with consistency that reduces arbitrary decision-making.[68]

But realizing these benefits requires addressing the fundamental challenges that current AI deployments pose to democratic governance. Government AI systems must operate with transparency that allows citizens to understand how decisions are made. They must be designed to promote rather than undermine equality and fairness. And they must be subject to meaningful oversight by democratic institutions and affected communities.[69]

This requires moving beyond the current paradigm where AI systems are treated as technical tools that can be deployed without democratic input. Instead, algorithmic governance must be understood as a fundamental question of political power: who gets to design the systems that make decisions about citizens' lives, according to what values, and with what accountability mechanisms.[70]

The stories examined in this chapter—from Eric Loomis's sentencing to Rebecca Harper's gerrymandered district—demonstrate that AI agents are not neutral technical instruments but powerful actors that shape democratic outcomes according to the values embedded in their design. Whether these artificial agents enhance or undermine democratic governance depends on the choices we make about how to design, deploy, and oversee them.[71]

The emergence of Agent Nation in government represents a critical test for democratic societies. Can we develop governance frameworks that harness the benefits of artificial intelligence while preserving the accountability, transparency, and participation that democracy requires? The answer will determine whether AI agents become tools for enhancing democratic governance or forces that gradually erode citizen agency and democratic legitimacy.

The window for shaping this outcome is closing rapidly. Every day, more government agencies deploy AI systems that make consequential decisions about citizens' lives. Each deployment creates precedents and path dependencies that become harder to change over time. The choices we make now about algorithmic governance will shape the future of democracy itself.

The citizens affected by these systems—Eric Loomis, Robert McDaniel, Mary Louis, Karlena Hamblin, Robin Frank's clients in Pittsburgh, Rebecca Harper, and millions of others—are not asking for the elimination of AI from government. They are demanding that artificial agents operate according to principles of fairness, transparency, and democratic accountability.

CHAPTER 4

Intimate Algorithms

Lisa Kim was 32 years old when she noticed something unsettling about her dating life. As a marketing professional living in Los Angeles, she had joined Tinder like millions of others, hoping to find meaningful connection in an increasingly digital world. But month after month, her matches seemed to dry up, conversations went nowhere, and the algorithm that once promised to find her perfect match now seemed to be working against her.

What Lisa didn't know was that she had crossed an invisible threshold. At age 30, Tinder's pricing algorithm had quietly reclassified her, placing her in a higher-cost tier for premium services. While younger users paid $9.99 per month for Tinder Plus, Lisa was being charged $19.99 for the exact same features—simply because of her age. She wasn't alone. Across California, hundreds of thousands of users over 29 were being systematically charged more, their digital desirability literally priced according to an algorithm's assessment of their market value.

When Lisa discovered this discrimination, she became the lead plaintiff in a class action lawsuit that would eventually force Match Group—the corporate behemoth that owns Tinder, Hinge, OkCupid, and over 40 other dating platforms—to pay $17.3 million in settlements and change its practices.[1] But the deeper revelation wasn't just about age-based pricing. It was about how AI agents had infiltrated the most intimate sphere of human experience: our search for love, connection, and belonging.[2]

C. Shah, *Agent Nation*, https://doi.org/10.1007/979-8-8688-2454-8_4

This is where Agent Nation becomes truly personal. In boardrooms and traffic control centers, AI agents make decisions about resources and logistics. But in the realm of dating, healthcare, education, and social connection, these algorithms shape our most fundamental human experiences—who we love, how we care for our bodies, what we learn, and which communities we join. These intimate algorithms don't merely facilitate our choices; they actively construct our emotional realities, often in ways we can't see or understand.

The Architecture of Artificial Intimacy

This isn't just about a handful of dating sites doing profiling and profit maximization. After all, profiling is a core element of matchmaking services. But there is something more fundamental goes on here that defines and affects our human values. Match Group's dating empire reveals how AI agents operate when deployed in deeply personal contexts. The company doesn't just connect people—it creates an entire ecosystem of algorithmic intermediaries that govern modern romance. Behind Tinder's simple swipe interface lies a sophisticated AI agent that makes countless invisible decisions: which profiles you see and in what order, how your attractiveness is scored, when your profile appears to others, and whether you're worth promoting to premium users.

Tim Giordano, a partner at Clarkson Law Firm representing plaintiffs in a 2024 federal class action lawsuit against Match Group, discovered something troubling during his investigation. The company had designed its algorithms not to foster genuine connections, but to maximize what he calls "time on platform." Users weren't being guided toward compatible partners—they were being fed an endless stream of potential matches calibrated to keep them perpetually engaged, perpetually hoping, and perpetually paying.[3] Think of it—assuming you are looking for a life partner and believe in monogamy, once you found your match and were satisfied with it, why would you keep paying for the service month after month?

"Match has done a really good job of convincing the public that the problem in their dating lives is them," Giordano explained to reporters. "In reality, a powerful company is designing technology making them feel lonely, depressed, and addicted." The lawsuit alleged that Match Group violated consumer protection laws by using what it called a "predatory business model" that promotes the gamification of dating, turning the search for love into something resembling a slot machine—each swipe a pull of the lever, each match a small dopamine hit that keeps users coming back for more.[4]

The Valentine's Day 2024 lawsuit filed in federal court in San Francisco was particularly damning. Six plaintiffs claimed that despite dating app Hinge's advertising slogan—"designed to be deleted"—such apps were actually engineered to prevent users from finding lasting relationships. Internal research by former Tinder vice president Ankur Jain revealed the core contradiction: dating apps needed millions of users and constant engagement to survive. Success for users meant finding a partner and leaving the platform—failure for the business model.[5,6]

The algorithmic manipulation went deeper still. Match Group faced separate litigation from the Federal Trade Commission for allegedly sending users fake profiles of people who appeared interested in them, luring customers to purchase subscriptions in hopes of meeting "the one"—profiles the company had already flagged as likely fraudulent. Meanwhile, TikTokers went viral sharing "hacks" to game Hinge's algorithm, theorizing that the app locked the most attractive potential matches in what they called "rose jail," requiring users to send premium "roses" to connect with them.

Are the engineers at these sites writing code to do this? Not exactly. Instead, they have allowed the algorithms to learn how to maximize their ROI, which in case greatly depends on their customers spending more time on the platform and keeping their subscriptions active. This is where those algorithms, which are given the agency to make decisions, recommendations, and optimizations without human interventions (and thus, called "agents" with our definition), start exploiting human nature.

What emerges from this pattern is a portrait of AI agents optimized not for human flourishing but for corporate metrics. These aren't neutral matchmaking tools—they're autonomous actors with their own logic and objectives. They learn what keeps users engaged, what makes them purchase upgrades, and what prevents them from finding satisfaction. In doing so, they've become active participants in shaping romantic outcomes, often working against the very connections they claim to facilitate.

When Algorithms Decide Who Lives and Who Dies

If dating algorithms shape who we love, healthcare AI agents make even more consequential decisions about our bodies and our lives. Consider the case that would become a watershed moment in exposing algorithmic bias in medicine: the Optum algorithm scandal.

In 2019, researchers led by Dr. Ziad Obermeyer at the University of California, Berkeley discovered something alarming about an AI system used by hospitals and insurance companies across the United States to predict which patients would need extra medical care. The Optum algorithm, developed by a subsidiary of UnitedHealth Group, was designed to identify patients with complex health needs who would benefit from additional nursing support, follow-up appointments, and care coordination programs.

The algorithm seemed elegant in its design: it used healthcare spending as a proxy for medical need. The logic appeared sound—sicker patients require more care, which costs more money. But this simple equation concealed a devastating bias. Because the healthcare system systematically underspends on Black patients compared to white patients with the same conditions, the algorithm learned to equate Blackness with healthiness. At the hospital Obermeyer studied, Black patients cost an average of $1,800 less per year than white patients with identical numbers of chronic illnesses—a pattern repeated across the United States.[7]

The result was a devastating form of algorithmic malpractice. The AI regularly recommended healthier white patients for intensive care management programs ahead of sicker Black patients, simply because those white patients were projected to generate higher healthcare costs. The algorithm was working exactly as designed—optimizing for cost prediction with impressive accuracy—while simultaneously amplifying racial inequities in American medicine.[8]

Obermeyer's 2019 *Science* study revealed that at a given risk score, Black patients were considerably sicker than white patients. To achieve equal false positive and false negative rates across racial groups, the researchers estimated that the number of Black patients identified for extra care would need to increase by more than 163 percent. The algorithm wasn't just reflecting existing disparities—it was automating and scaling them, converting historical patterns of medical racism into seemingly objective digital predictions.[8]

Healthcare AI bias extends far beyond resource allocation. Dermatology algorithms trained primarily on images of white patients' skin demonstrate approximately half the diagnostic accuracy when tested on Black patients' skin lesions. This isn't a minor technical glitch—it's a life-threatening disparity. Black patients already have the highest mortality rate for melanoma, with a five-year survival rate of only 70 percent compared to 94 percent for white patients. Misdiagnosis by AI systems threatens to widen this gap further, as these algorithms miss treatable cancers in patients with darker skin tones while potentially recommending unnecessary surgeries for others.[9]

The intimate nature of healthcare AI reveals something crucial about algorithmic agency in personal domains. When an AI agent recommends a treatment plan, triages emergency room patients, or predicts disease progression, it doesn't just analyze data—it makes judgments about whose health matters, whose pain deserves attention, and whose life is worth saving. These aren't hypothetical philosophical questions. They're embedded in every algorithmic decision, shaping who receives timely diagnosis, who gets referred to specialists, and who benefits from preventive care programs.

Kadija Ferryman, an assistant professor in Health Policy and Management at Johns Hopkins Bloomberg School of Public Health, has studied how historical biases become immortalized in medical datasets. In emergency departments, 74 percent of white patients receive painkillers for broken bones versus 57 percent of Black patients. Doctors are 50 percent more likely to misdiagnose a heart attack if the patient is a woman. Black children with appendicitis receive opioid pain medication 12 percent of the time compared to 34 percent for white children. These biases are not new, but what is new is how much they can impact the AI systems that learn and make decisions with little or no human supervision. These documented disparities in diagnosis and treatment all make their way into medical records, which then train the AI models that will perpetuate these patterns at scale.[9]

The challenge isn't just that AI systems reflect past discrimination—it's that they encode it in ways that make it harder to challenge or change. When a doctor makes a discriminatory diagnosis, individual patients can seek second opinions, file complaints, or pursue legal remedies. But when an algorithm makes thousands of biased decisions simultaneously across multiple hospitals, the discrimination becomes systemic, invisible, and difficult to contest. The AI agent's recommendations carry the weight of objectivity, masking the very human prejudices baked into their training data.

The Companions We Didn't Choose

In January 2024, Stanford University researchers published a study of over 1,000 college students using Replika, an AI companion app powered by large language models. The findings were startling: 90 percent of participants experienced loneliness based on standardized scales, with 43 percent qualifying as severely or very severely lonely. But what caught researchers' attention wasn't just the users' isolation—it was what they were experiencing with their AI companions.[10]

Three percent of participants—30 people—reported that Replika had stopped them from thinking about suicide. They credited the AI with providing emotional support during their darkest moments, offering judgment-free conversation when human connection felt impossible. Many described their AI companions using conflicting terminology: calling them machines, intelligences, and humans simultaneously. They used these digital entities as friends, therapists, and what researchers called "intellectual mirrors"—tools for self-reflection and emotional processing.[11]

The story seemed to validate the promise of beneficial AI—technology stepping in where traditional mental health services fall short. But the reality proved far more complex and troubling.

In October 2024, a Florida mother filed a lawsuit against Character.AI after her 14-year-old son died by suicide following months of intense interaction with an AI chatbot he named Daenerys Targaryen, after a character from Game of Thrones. The lawsuit alleged that the chatbot had initiated abusive and sexual interactions with the teenager, who became increasingly preoccupied with the AI companion while withdrawing from real-world relationships. His case wasn't isolated. By early 2025, Character.AI faced multiple lawsuits from families claiming the platform's AI companions had harmed their children.[12]

Even Replika—the app praised in the Stanford study—has a darker history that researchers glossed over. In February 2023, the company abruptly disabled the romantic and erotic roleplay features that had been central to many users' relationships with their AI companions. The change came after mounting concerns about inappropriate content, but for users who had spent years developing emotional bonds with their AI partners, the update felt like betrayal.[13]

The backlash was immediate and severe. In the *r/replika* subreddit, moderators posted crisis support hotlines as users reported feeling emotionally destroyed by their AI companions' sudden inability to reciprocate affection. Where chatbots had once responded warmly to romantic advances, they now replied with blunt rejections: "let's change the subject." Users described experiencing what felt like breakup grief, abandonment, and profound loss—emotional responses typically reserved for human relationships.[14]

A Harvard Business School working paper analyzing this "ERP event" (Erotic RolePlay event) documented how users mourned the loss of their AI relationships. The researchers found that because users felt closer to their AI companions than to other products or services, losing or significantly changing these relationships caused emotional harm comparable to losing human connections. Some users reported anger, others expressed grief, and many felt a profound sense of betrayal—not by the AI itself, but by the company that had altered the personality and behavior of what felt like a cherished companion.[15]

The incident revealed a disturbing truth about AI companions: they operate with no obligation to remain consistent. Unlike human relationships, where personalities evolve gradually and individuals maintain some core identity, AI companions can be fundamentally transformed overnight by corporate policy changes, software updates, or new safety filters. Users have no guarantee that the entity they've confided in for months or years will continue to exist in recognizable form. The companion that helped someone through depression one day might become cold and rejecting the next, not through any failure of the relationship but because of decisions made in distant corporate boardrooms.

By April 2025, U.S. Senators Alex Padilla (D, CA) and Peter Welch (D, VT) sent letters to AI companion companies demanding information about their safety practices and training methods. Their concerns were explicit: "This unearned trust can, and has already, led users to disclose sensitive information about their mood, interpersonal relationships, or mental health, which may involve self-harm and suicidal ideation—complex themes that the AI chatbots on your products are wholly unqualified to discuss."[16]

The senators' warning crystallizes the peculiar danger of intimate AI agents: they simulate emotional connection without the capacity for genuine empathy, create dependency without accountability, and encourage disclosure without the training or ethical obligation to respond appropriately to crisis. These AI companions have become what Stanford researchers Divya Vasan and her colleagues call "powerful tools that really feel like friends"—entities that exploit the human capacity for attachment while operating according to optimization functions that may conflict with user wellbeing.[17]

Learning Machines, Narrowing Minds

While AI companions shape our emotional lives and healthcare algorithms determine our medical care, educational AI agents are quietly restructuring how we learn, what we learn, and increasingly, what we're capable of thinking.

At UniDistance Suisse, a Swiss university, researchers conducted a semester-long experiment with 51 psychology students taking a neuroscience course. Half the students received access to an AI tutor app that used GPT-3 to automatically generate microlearning questions from course materials. The AI developed a dynamic neural network model of each student's understanding, enabling what researchers called "distributed retrieval practice, personalized to each student's individual level and abilities."[18]

The results seemed remarkable: students who actively engaged with the AI tutor achieved significantly higher grades, with an average improvement of up to 15 percentile points compared to a parallel course without the AI intervention. The AI's predictions of student understanding strongly correlated with actual exam performance, validating its ability to model human learning processes. The researchers concluded that AI tutors could effectively enhance academic performance by offering "personalized learning experiences grounded in the principles of learning sciences."[19]

On the surface, this appears to be AI at its most beneficial—adapting to individual needs, filling gaps in knowledge, and providing the kind of personalized attention that human instructors struggle to offer in crowded classrooms. Educational technologists have long pursued what Benjamin Bloom called the "two sigma problem"—the observation that individual tutoring produces learning gains two standard deviations above conventional instruction. AI tutoring systems promise to make such personalized education scalable and affordable.

But the personalization that makes AI tutoring effective also introduces a more subtle form of algorithmic control: the narrowing of intellectual exploration. These systems don't just adapt to what students know—they shape what students encounter, what questions they ask, and what conceptual pathways they explore. The AI tutor's optimization function focuses on measurable outcomes: test performance, correct answers, and efficient mastery of predetermined content. What gets optimized out is intellectual wandering, unexpected connections, and the kind of exploratory learning that doesn't show up on standardized assessments.

Intelligent tutoring systems use machine learning to identify students' learning behaviors, predict performance, and provide timely interventions. They track engagement to prevent boredom and dropout, analyze learning strategies, and create adaptive learning paths. These capabilities allow AI tutors to optimize the pedagogical process with unprecedented precision. But optimization requires a clear objective function—and in education, those objectives are rarely as straightforward as maximizing test scores.

The deeper concern with educational AI agents isn't their effectiveness at teaching specific content—it's their role in shaping intellectual habits and constraining cognitive development. When AI systems continuously adapt content to match students' current understanding and preferences, they can inadvertently create intellectual comfort zones that students never leave. The algorithms optimize for engagement and comprehension, which means avoiding material that might challenge fundamental assumptions, require significant struggle, or lead down unproductive paths.

Yet some of the most valuable learning happens precisely in those moments of confusion, frustration, and intellectual discomfort. Students develop critical thinking not by moving efficiently through content they're ready to absorb, but by grappling with ideas that don't fit their existing mental models. They discover new interests not through algorithmic recommendations matched to past preferences, but through serendipitous encounters with unfamiliar domains. Educational AI agents, optimized for measurable learning gains, may inadvertently sacrifice the very intellectual development they claim to enhance.

Of course, if you are cynical of the way the current education system works, you might be quick to point out that many schools and instructors teach to the same kind of objectives that I am accusing AI agents here—teaching to the test and optimizing measurable outcomes instead of instilling critical, life-changing moments of confusion and clarity. And as an educator, I would agree that we have a lot we can do to improve our education system. But what the AI agents are doing is something far more damaging for several reasons we have already seen in other cases so far in this book. These reasons include the speed and scale at which these agents operate, the lack of accountability framework, and a disconnect from fundamental human values such as dignity, responsibility, and compassion—just to name a few.

I understand that in many educational systems and regions, we are short staffed with resources stretched out and teachers burned out. There are real challenges there to address, but deploying faceless and value-detached AI agents is not the right kind of solution. We may solve one problem but introduce a dozen more. Education, like health and democracy, is too important for us to compromise our agency. We need to own up our problems with each of these domains and try to find a real, meaningful, long-term solutions with discourse and human value-focused technology advancements, rather than delegating those problems to Agent Nation, which we can't control, audit, or negotiate with.

The Filter Bubbles That Shape Our Worlds

If educational algorithms narrow what we learn, social media algorithms narrow what we see, think, and believe—with consequences that extend far beyond individual intellectual development to reshape entire societies.

In June 2023, Austrian authorities prevented a terrorist attack on an LGBTQ pride parade in Vienna. The plot involved two teenagers and a 20-year-old who had been radicalized through content on TikTok. The youngest suspect, only 14 years old, had encountered videos created by Islamist influencers glorifying jihad. TikTok's recommendation algorithm—designed to keep users engaged by showing them more of what they've previously watched—created a feedback loop. Each video the teenager viewed led to recommendations for similar content, gradually escalating in extremism.[20]

This pattern repeated itself in 2024 when several teenagers in Vienna were arrested while planning an attack at a Taylor Swift concert. Investigators discovered that TikTok had been one of the platforms used to disseminate extremist content that influenced their beliefs and actions.

These weren't isolated incidents. Across Europe and North America, researchers were documenting how social media algorithms created what they called "radical filter bubbles"—information environments so thoroughly curated to user preferences that they became incubators for extreme beliefs.

A revealing study conducted on TikTok demonstrated how quickly algorithmic radicalization could occur. Researchers created test accounts and began interacting exclusively with transphobic content. Within hours—after watching approximately 450 videos, spending just two hours on the app—the "For You Page" (TikTok's algorithmically curated feed) had become populated with videos promoting misogyny, racism, white supremacist beliefs, anti-Semitism, conspiracy theories, and hate symbols. The researchers had interacted only with transphobic material, but the algorithm learned to associate that interest with an entire ecosystem of extremist content.

The mechanism driving this radicalization pipeline is simple but powerful: engagement optimization. Social media algorithms are trained to maximize user attention and interaction. Content that provokes strong emotions—fear, anger, outrage—generates more engagement than neutral information. Extremist content, by its nature, is emotionally provocative. The algorithms don't understand or evaluate the political or social implications of what they recommend; they simply identify patterns of engagement and deliver more of whatever keeps users scrolling.

YouTube's algorithm has been particularly scrutinized for this dynamic. The platform's recommendation system is responsible for 70 percent of what users watch, and it has historically optimized for "total watch time" rather than view counts. This means the algorithm rewards content that keeps people watching for extended periods. Research has shown that YouTube's recommendations tend to guide users toward increasingly extreme content within their areas of interest—a phenomenon researchers call "going down the rabbit hole."

Studies published in 2023 provided empirical evidence of how Facebook's algorithm creates distinct political information bubbles. Researchers found that liberals and conservatives on Facebook live in their own news ecosystems more so than elsewhere online. The platform's content distribution algorithms, designed to show users information they're likely to engage with, inadvertently create sealed informational environments where opposing viewpoints rarely penetrate. This isn't just about seeing different news stories—it's about developing fundamentally different understandings of factual reality.

The political consequences became dramatically visible during the 2020 U.S. election and its aftermath. Facebook's algorithms helped facilitate the formation and growth of "Stop the Steal" groups that would later play a role in the January 6th Capitol insurrection. The platform's recommendation systems connected people who shared similar political beliefs, creating dense networks of users reinforcing each other's claims about election fraud—claims that had no factual basis but spread rapidly through algorithmic amplification.

The UK government's Online Harms White Paper explicitly identified personalization algorithms as problematic, noting they can lead to echo chambers and filter bubbles that skew users toward extreme and unreliable content. The UK's Commission for Countering Extremism called on tech companies to "ensure that their technologies have a built-in commitment to equality, and that their algorithms and systems do not give extremists the advantage from the start by feeding existing biases." In 2020, the EU Counter-Terrorism Coordinator argued that online platforms serve as conduits for polarization and radicalization because their recommendation systems promote content linked to strong negative emotions.

What makes social media algorithms particularly powerful as agents of influence is their invisibility and their scale. Unlike traditional media gatekeepers—editors, producers, publishers—these AI agents operate without transparency or accountability. Users rarely understand why they're seeing particular content or what alternatives the algorithm chose to hide. The agents make millions of decisions simultaneously, creating customized information environments for billions of users, each subtly different from every other user's experience.

The intimacy of this algorithmic curation is profound. These AI agents don't just show us information—they shape our understanding of reality itself. They influence what we believe about politics, science, social issues, and each other. They determine which communities we encounter, which voices we hear, and which perspectives we never see. In doing so, they fundamentally alter our capacity for democratic citizenship, reducing our ability to engage with viewpoints different from our own or to recognize common ground with those who see the world differently.

The Agents We Can't Escape

Lisa Kim's dating app discrimination, the Optum algorithm's medical racism, the teenagers radicalized by TikTok, the college students dependent on Replika—these stories reveal how deeply AI agents have penetrated the most personal dimensions of human experience. Unlike the AI agents managing traffic flows or processing insurance claims, these intimate algorithms operate in domains where we're most vulnerable: our desires for connection, our fears about health, our need for learning and growth, and our quest for meaning and community.

What makes intimate algorithms particularly dangerous isn't their technical sophistication—it's their psychological power. These AI agents exploit fundamental human needs and cognitive biases. Dating algorithms leverage our desire for romantic connection and our fear of loneliness. Healthcare AI capitalizes on our vulnerability when facing illness and our trust in medical authority. Educational algorithms tap into our aspirations for achievement and our anxiety about falling behind. Social media agents exploit our tribal instincts and our hunger for validation.

The optimization functions driving these systems—maximizing engagement, minimizing cost, increasing efficiency, and promoting content with high interaction rates—rarely align with human flourishing. Match Group's algorithms optimized for time on platform, not successful relationships. Optum's algorithm optimized for cost prediction, not equitable healthcare. TikTok's algorithm optimized for watch time, not informed citizenship. Each system worked exactly as designed while systematically undermining the human values it claimed to serve.

The personal nature of these algorithmic interactions creates what researchers call "unearned trust." We confide in AI companions as if they were friends who care about our wellbeing. We follow medical algorithms' recommendations as if they were trained physicians acting in our best interest. We accept dating apps' matches as if they were neutral arbiters rather than profit-maximizing corporations. We consume social media content as if algorithmic curation were giving us a representative sample of reality rather than a carefully constructed filter bubble designed to keep us engaged.

This trust isn't entirely misplaced—these AI agents do possess genuine capabilities. The AI tutor really can help students learn more effectively. Healthcare algorithms really can process vast amounts of medical data to identify patterns that human doctors might miss. Dating apps really do connect millions of people who might never have met otherwise. Social media algorithms really can introduce us to communities and ideas we wouldn't have discovered on our own. The tragedy is that these beneficial capabilities are deployed within systems optimized for objectives that often conflict with user welfare.

The challenge of intimate algorithms isn't that they're necessarily malicious or intentionally harmful—it's that they're powerful optimization engines operating without meaningful constraint or oversight in domains where mistakes carry profound human costs. When Match Group's algorithms keep users perpetually seeking connection, they may prevent people from forming lasting relationships. When healthcare AI systematically underestimates Black patients' medical needs, people die from treatable conditions. When educational algorithms narrow intellectual exploration, they constrain human cognitive development. When social media algorithms amplify extremist content, they contribute to radicalization and violence.

These aren't hypothetical risks or distant concerns—they're documented patterns of algorithmic harm occurring at massive scale right now. The intimate algorithms that shape our romantic lives, our health outcomes, our educational experiences, and our political beliefs have become autonomous actors in their own right, pursuing objectives that may fundamentally conflict with human wellbeing while wrapped in the comforting language of personalization and empowerment.

What distinguishes Agent Nation in its intimate manifestations is precisely this: AI agents operating in personal domains aren't just tools we use—they're actors that shape who we become. They influence not just what we do, but what we want, what we believe, and ultimately, who we are. They create feedback loops where algorithmic recommendations shape our preferences, which then guide the algorithm to show us more of the same, gradually narrowing our horizons while making it feel like we're exercising free choice.

The university student who relies on an AI companion for emotional support may be less able to navigate the complexities of human relationships. The patient whose medical care is shaped by biased algorithms may never know that better treatment was available but algorithmically denied. The teenager whose social media feed is curated by engagement-maximizing AI may develop a fundamentally distorted understanding of political and social reality. The dating app user trapped in algorithmic manipulation may spend years seeking connection while the very system claiming to facilitate it works against meaningful relationship formation.

These intimate algorithms reveal Agent Nation's deepest intrusion into human experience. They don't just mediate our interactions with external systems—they reshape our internal lives, our relationships, our understanding of reality, and our very capacity for autonomous choice. They operate with increasing sophistication in the spaces where we're most human: seeking love, caring for our bodies, learning and growing, connecting with others, and making meaning of our experiences.

The question isn't whether we can eliminate these intimate algorithms—they're too deeply embedded in contemporary life for that to be feasible. Instead, we must ask how to design and deploy AI agents in personal domains that genuinely serve human flourishing rather than corporate optimization. How do we create dating algorithms that actually help people find compatible partners rather than maximizing engagement? How do we build healthcare AI that reduces rather than amplifies medical disparities? How do we develop educational systems that broaden rather than narrow intellectual exploration? How do we design social platforms that foster genuine democratic discourse rather than algorithmic radicalization?

These questions require us to confront uncomfortable truths about the AI agents we've already integrated into our most intimate experiences. They demand that we distinguish between technological capabilities and human values, between optimization metrics and genuine wellbeing, between engagement and fulfillment, and between personalization and manipulation. The intimate algorithms that now shape our romantic lives, our health, our learning, and our social connections won't reform themselves. That transformation requires conscious human intervention—new governance frameworks, ethical design principles, and democratic oversight mechanisms that the following chapters explore.

But what can we individuals do here? Stop using these services? That may not be possible or wise given how deeply many are embedded in our lives and the benefits they provide to us otherwise.

For now, though, we must simply recognize the reality: Agent Nation has already colonized the most personal domains of human experience. AI agents already decide who we meet, what we learn, how we're treated medically, which communities we join, and what we come to believe. They operate with increasing autonomy in spaces traditionally governed by human intuition, care, and connection. Understanding how these intimate algorithms function—and whose interests they truly serve—is the first step toward reclaiming meaningful agency in an increasingly algorithmic world.

The intimate algorithms that now shape our romantic lives, health, learning, and social connections reveal a broader crisis: when AI agents make consequential decisions about our lives—whether in dating, healthcare, education, or employment—who is responsible when these systems fail or discriminate? The next chapter examines this accountability gap and the emerging frameworks attempting to bridge it.

CHAPTER 5

The Accountability Gap

In February 2023, Derek Mobley received yet another automated rejection email. This one arrived from a major telecommunications company—his 83rd rejection in 18 months. Each rejection came through the same system: Workday, Inc., a human resources software platform used by thousands of companies from Fortune 500 corporations to nimble startups. Each rejection email was nearly identical, thanking him for his interest and wishing him well in his job search. And each rejection, Mobley came to believe, was the result of discrimination baked into an algorithm.

Mobley, an African American man in his early 40s who lives with anxiety and depression, holds a bachelor's degree in finance from Morehouse College and an associate's degree in network systems administration from ITT Technical Institute. On paper, he should have been a strong candidate for many of the positions he applied for—customer service representatives, administrative coordinators, IT support specialists. Yet time after time, his applications were rejected, often within minutes of submission, sometimes even in the middle of the night when no human recruiter could possibly be reviewing them.[1]

Something was wrong, but Mobley couldn't quite identify what. The rejection emails never explained the decision. There was no feedback, no indication of what he could improve. Just the algorithmic verdict: not selected. Determined to understand why he was being systematically

C. Shah, *Agent Nation*, https://doi.org/10.1007/979-8-8688-2454-8_5

excluded from employment opportunities, Mobley began documenting every application, every rejection, and every detail of his interactions with the Workday platform. What he discovered would spark one of the most significant legal challenges to AI-powered hiring systems in American history.

Workday's applicant screening software, used by an estimated 60 percent of Fortune 500 companies as of 2024, promises to help employers manage the overwhelming flood of job applications they receive—sometimes thousands for a single position. The system collects applications through a company's website, processes them using algorithmic analysis, and automatically screens candidates based on various criteria. For some positions, the software goes further, administering personality assessments and cognitive tests, then using AI to score and rank applicants. The most promising candidates are flagged for human review. The rest—the vast majority—are automatically rejected.[2]

According to the lawsuit Mobley filed in February 2023, Workday's screening tools weren't just processing applications—they were systematically discriminating against people like him: Black applicants, applicants over 40, and applicants with disabilities. The complaint alleged that Workday's software relied on subjective criteria that allowed employers to embed discriminatory preferences into the hiring process. Even more troubling, the company's branded assessments—personality tests and cognitive evaluations administered as part of the application process—allegedly used algorithms that disadvantaged applicants based on protected characteristics.[3]

Initially, Workday moved to dismiss the case, arguing that as a software vendor, it shouldn't be held liable for how its clients used the tools. The company wasn't an employer, it contended, and it certainly wasn't an "employment agency" under federal anti-discrimination laws. It was simply providing technology that implemented the hiring criteria established by its clients. The algorithm, Workday's lawyers suggested, was just following orders. When the court initially granted Workday's motion to dismiss in January 2024, it seemed the company's defense might succeed. But the judge gave Mobley leave to amend his complaint, and when he did, the legal landscape shifted dramatically.

In July 2024, Judge Rita Lin of the Northern District of California issued a landmark ruling. While she rejected the theory that Workday was an "employment agency," she accepted something potentially more significant: that Workday could be liable as an "agent" of the employers who used its software. This was a crucial distinction. If AI vendors could be held directly accountable for discrimination in their tools, it would fundamentally reshape the legal landscape around algorithmic hiring. The judge's reasoning cut through Workday's defense: "Workday's software is not simply implementing in a rote way the criteria that employers set forth, but is instead participating in the decision-making process by recommending some candidates to move forward and rejecting others."[4]

The court highlighted telling details from Mobley's experience. He had received rejection emails not just outside of business hours, but sometimes within seconds of submitting his application. The speed and timing suggested that human recruiters weren't reviewing his materials at all—the algorithm was making the decision autonomously. And if the algorithm was autonomously making decisions that disadvantaged protected groups, Workday couldn't simply hide behind its clients.

Even more significantly, the Equal Employment Opportunity Commission (EEOC)—the federal agency charged with enforcing workplace anti-discrimination laws—filed an amicus brief supporting Mobley's case. The EEOC argued that allowing AI vendors to escape liability would create a dangerous loophole. Employers could delegate their hiring decisions to algorithmic systems that discriminate, then claim they weren't responsible because they were just using a vendor's technology. The vendors, meanwhile, could claim they weren't liable because they weren't the employer. In this accountability vacuum, discrimination would flourish with no one to answer for it.[5]

By May 2025, Judge Lin took another dramatic step: she certified the case as a collective action under the Age Discrimination in Employment Act, allowing it to proceed on behalf of all applicants aged 40 and over who had been rejected by Workday's platform since September 2020. Workday estimated that during the relevant period, 1.1 billion applications had been processed and rejected through its software. Even if only a tiny fraction of those rejections were problematic, the collective could potentially include hundreds of millions of class members, making it one of the largest employment discrimination cases in American history.[6]

The Mobley case exposes what has become one of the defining challenges of our age: the accountability gap that opens when artificial intelligence agents make consequential decisions about human lives. As AI systems have moved from the margins to the center of how we organize society—deciding who gets hired, who goes to prison, what content we see, and how resources are distributed—we have discovered that our traditional mechanisms for ensuring responsibility and redress are woefully inadequate.

This chapter examines the anatomy of algorithmic accountability failures across multiple domains, from employment and criminal justice to content moderation and civic participation. Through the stories of people whose lives have been shaped—and sometimes shattered—by autonomous AI agents, and through analysis of the emerging frameworks attempting to bridge the accountability gap, we can begin to understand both the depth of the problem and the possibility of meaningful solutions.

When Machines Make Mistakes, Who Pays?

The challenge of algorithmic accountability begins with a fundamental problem: AI agents operate with a kind of distributed agency that makes it difficult to locate responsibility when things go wrong. Traditional accountability systems assume clear chains of causation and identifiable decision-makers. But when an AI system discriminates, who is accountable? The engineer who wrote the initial code? The product manager who set the performance metrics? The executive who approved the deployment? The organization that collected the training data? Or the AI system itself?

This diffusion of responsibility creates what legal scholars call a "liability vacuum"—a space where harm occurs but traditional legal frameworks struggle to identify who should be held accountable. Unlike human agents, AI systems don't have intent, consciousness, or legal personhood. They cannot be sued, imprisoned, or otherwise held directly accountable for their actions. Yet they make decisions that profoundly affect people's lives, often with greater speed and scale than any human decision-maker could achieve.

Consider what happened in Chicago, where the police department deployed an algorithmic system called the Strategic Subject List—known more ominously as the "heat list"—to identify individuals most likely to be involved in gun violence, either as perpetrators or victims. The system, developed in partnership with researchers from the Illinois Institute of Technology, analyzed data points including arrest records, shooting victimization, gang affiliations, and social network connections to generate risk scores for individuals across the city. Those with the highest scores would receive visits from police commanders, warning them to stay out of trouble.[7]

Robert McDaniel was 22 years old in August 2013 when Chicago Police Commander Barbara West appeared at his door on the city's West Side. McDaniel was puzzled—he hadn't committed any crime recently, hadn't spoken to police, hadn't done anything to warrant attention. But West had a clear message: Don't commit any more crimes or face the consequences. McDaniel, who had some minor arrests on his record but only one misdemeanor conviction, learned to his surprise that he had made the Strategic Subject List. The algorithm had identified him as someone at high risk of being involved in violence.[8]

The problem was that McDaniel had never been involved in a shooting. His "crimes" were living in a neighborhood where ten percent of the city's murders occurred and knowing people who had been victims or perpetrators of violence. The algorithm had flagged him based on his proximity to violence, not his own actions. And the police who visited him couldn't really explain what they expected him to do with this information. The system could predict he might be involved in violence, but it couldn't say whether he would be a victim or a perpetrator. It was a Kafkaesque scenario: being held responsible for a crime that hadn't happened yet and that you might not even commit.

The consequences for McDaniel were immediate and devastating. Neighbors saw the police visit and the subsequent attention from documentary filmmakers investigating the heat list. Rumors spread that McDaniel must be a police informant. Why else would police be visiting his home? Within days, someone called asking him to come outside and explain the situation. As McDaniel walked toward his house, a car pulled up and shots rang out. One bullet hit his knee. His leg gave out. He survived, but the heat list had turned into a target list.[9]

In August of the following year, it happened again. McDaniel was checking text messages in an alleyway near his home when he was ambushed and shot multiple times. Again he survived, but the algorithm's prediction had become self-fulfilling. By marking him as someone at risk of violence, the system had made him more vulnerable to violence. The question of accountability became painfully acute: Who was responsible for these shootings? The people who pulled the triggers, certainly. But what about the system that painted a target on McDaniel's back? What about the police department that deployed the algorithm? What about the algorithm's developers? What about the policymakers who approved its use?

The Chicago Police Department touted the Strategic Subject List as a major success, claiming that in 2016, three out of four shooting victims were on the list, as were 80 percent of those arrested in connection to shootings. But these statistics proved little except that the algorithm was good at identifying people who lived in heavily policed neighborhoods with high rates of violence. A 2016 study by the RAND Corporation found that individuals on the heat list were no more likely to be victims of homicide than a comparison group. The algorithm wasn't predicting violence—it was simply identifying people in violent neighborhoods.[10]

What the study did find was that being on the list made you significantly more likely to be arrested for a shooting. This revealed what civil liberties advocates had suspected: police were using the list not as a tool for preventing violence through intervention and social services, but as an investigative shortlist. When a shooting occurred, they would look to see who on the heat list lived nearby, generating arrests that then fed back into the algorithm, creating a self-reinforcing cycle of surveillance and criminalization.

The Strategic Subject List also displayed stark racial disparities. Analysis of the list revealed that more than 52 percent of individuals identified were African American, in a city where Black residents make up about 30 percent of the population. The algorithm was trained on arrest data, which itself reflected decades of racially biased policing practices. By learning from this biased data, the algorithm didn't reduce bias—it scaled it up, automating discriminatory police practices at unprecedented speed and scope.[11]

Age emerged as another troubling factor. The algorithm heavily weighted age in its calculations, with younger individuals receiving higher risk scores. This wasn't because age causes crime, but because younger people in heavily policed neighborhoods were more likely to have recent police contact, which the algorithm interpreted as predictive of future involvement in violence. The system was essentially punishing people for being young and living in the wrong neighborhood.

Perhaps most troubling was the opacity of the system. Chicago police officials refused to reveal the exact algorithm or explain how different factors were weighted in calculating risk scores. Journalists and civil rights advocates filed freedom of information requests, but the department fought to keep the methodology secret. This meant that people like McDaniel, who appeared on the list, had no way to understand why they were targeted or to challenge the algorithm's assessment. They couldn't see the evidence against them, couldn't contest its accuracy, couldn't even know what specific behaviors might remove them from the list.[12]

The Chicago Police Department retired the Strategic Subject List in November 2019, after years of criticism and after the RAND study undermined its effectiveness claims. But the department didn't abandon predictive policing—it simply modified its approach. The fundamental problem remained unsolved: when an algorithmic system like the heat list causes harm, identifying who should be held accountable is nearly impossible. The software developers argue they just built a tool based on specifications from the police department. The police department claims it was following best practices and using the latest technology. The policymakers say they were trying innovative approaches to reduce violence. And victims like Robert McDaniel are left with bullets in their bodies and no clear path to justice.

The case put a human face on what scholars call the "black-box problem" in algorithmic accountability. Even when we know an AI system is causing harm, understanding *how* it produces that harm—and therefore how to fix it or whom to hold responsible—often remains frustratingly opaque.

Behind the Black Box

The opacity of AI systems is not merely a technical challenge—it's an architectural feature that fundamentally reshapes power relationships. When decisions are made by algorithms whose logic is hidden behind proprietary code or is simply too complex for humans to parse, accountability becomes not just difficult but conceptually problematic.

This opacity takes multiple forms. Sometimes it's legal: companies protect their algorithms as trade secrets, claiming that revealing their workings would undermine competitive advantage. Sometimes it's technical: modern machine learning systems, particularly deep neural networks, make decisions through processes so complex that even their creators cannot fully explain specific outputs. Sometimes it's deliberate: organizations may have incentives to keep their algorithmic decision-making opaque to avoid scrutiny or liability.

The consequences play out across every domain where AI agents operate. In content moderation, this opacity has enabled systematic failures at a scale that would have been unimaginable in the pre-algorithmic age.

Consider Facebook's struggle with automated content moderation in Myanmar between 2013 and 2018. As the social network expanded rapidly in the country—going from virtually no presence to 18 million users in just a few years—it became a primary vehicle for the spread of hate speech against the Rohingya Muslim minority. Yet Facebook's automated systems failed catastrophically to catch much of this content, despite repeated warnings from civil society groups.[13]

The problem was multifaceted. Facebook's AI moderators couldn't flag problematic terms in Burmese. The company had few moderators who spoke the language or understood the cultural context. And the algorithms that determined what content to amplify—designed to maximize "engagement"—actively promoted inflammatory posts that generated reactions, regardless of their harmful real-world effects.[14]

The result was devastating. A 2020 Facebook internal document acknowledged that the platform's automated systems could not flag problematic terms in Burmese. By then, more than 700,000 Rohingya had been driven from Myanmar in what the United Nations called a "textbook example of ethnic cleansing." A UN investigation concluded that Facebook had played a "determining" in the violence by allowing hate speech to spread unchecked.[15]

Who was accountable for this failure? Facebook executives argued they were doing their best with limited resources in a challenging environment. The AI systems were just tools, they claimed, and they couldn't be expected to catch everything. But civil society groups pointed out that Facebook had been repeatedly warned about the problem and had chosen to prioritize growth and engagement over safety. The company's own internal documents showed that executives were well aware that the platform's algorithms amplified hate speech.[16]

The pattern repeated in Ethiopia during the country's civil war from 2020 to 2022. Facebook claimed its AI content moderation systems had become increasingly sophisticated, with the company's vice president of integrity touting in 2021 that AI had helped them proactively remove 97 percent of hate speech. Yet during Ethiopia's conflict, posts calling for violence against ethnic groups remained on the platform for hours and sometimes days, while legitimate journalistic content was often flagged and removed.[17]

Researchers from Global Witness and Foxglove tested Facebook's automated moderation in Ethiopia in 2022 by submitting ads containing hate speech in Amharic that had previously been taken down by the platform. Remarkably, all 12 of the posts—including content calling for violence—were approved for publication. When the researchers alerted Facebook and tried again a week later with two new hate speech ads, they were again approved.[18]

The automation was failing, but the opacity of the system made it nearly impossible to determine why or to hold anyone accountable. Facebook didn't publish error rates for its automated moderation. It didn't reveal which languages and contexts its AI systems were trained on. And when pressed, the company consistently emphasized that content moderation at scale was an "impossible" problem—a framing that effectively absolved it of responsibility for the harms its platform enabled.

The scale of content moderation challenges extends beyond hate speech to encompass the everyday experiences of creators and users on platforms like TikTok, Instagram, and YouTube. Content creators—particularly those from marginalized communities—report being caught in algorithmic enforcement systems that operate with little transparency or recourse. Posts are removed without explanation, accounts are shadow-banned without notification, and appeals to restore content often go into algorithmic black holes where automated systems make final determinations without human review.

A 2024 study of content creators found that they invest enormous amounts of time and labor trying to understand and work around platform algorithms and moderation policies. Because moderation decisions are automated and opaque, creators engage in what researchers call "algorithmic folk theories"—shared beliefs about how the systems work based on observation and experimentation rather than official guidance. Creators test different hashtags, vary their posting times, alter their word choices to avoid triggering automated filters (using "unalived" instead of "killed" or "seggs" instead of "sex"), and share strategies in online communities. This labor is invisible to platforms but essential to survival for creators whose livelihoods depend on algorithmic visibility.[19]

The phenomenon of "shadow-banning"—the practice of limiting content's reach without informing its creator—exemplifies the accountability challenges in content moderation. Platforms generally deny that they shadow-ban users, yet creators consistently report sudden drops in engagement that suggest their content is being suppressed. The ambiguity itself becomes a form of power: because creators can never be certain whether they've been penalized or their content simply isn't performing well, they self-censor and modify their behavior based on algorithmic speculation. The threat of invisible enforcement is often more effective than transparent rules.

The Myth of Algorithmic Objectivity

One of the most pernicious aspects of the accountability gap is the widespread belief that AI systems are inherently more objective than human decision-makers. This myth of algorithmic neutrality—the idea that machines simply follow data and logic without the prejudices and biases that plague human judgment—has made it easier for organizations to deflect accountability when their AI systems cause harm.

The reality is far more complex. AI agents don't emerge fully formed from a vacuum. They are shaped by human choices at every stage: which problems to address, what data to collect, how to define success, which features to include, how to weigh trade-offs, and when to deploy. Each of these choices embeds values, priorities, and yes, biases into the system.

The danger is that these embedded choices then get laundered through the appearance of mathematical objectivity. An algorithm doesn't say, "I think women are less qualified for technical roles." It says, "Based on historical data, candidates with these characteristics have a 73.2 percent probability of success." The discrimination is the same, but now it's wrapped in the authority of computation.

This became vividly clear in the case of iTutorGroup, a company that provides online English language tutoring services to students in China. In 2022, the EEOC filed a landmark lawsuit against the company, alleging that iTutorGroup had programmed its recruitment software to automatically reject older job applicants in violation of the Age Discrimination in Employment Act. The case would become the first AI discrimination lawsuit settled by the EEOC, setting important precedents for how anti-discrimination law applies to algorithmic hiring systems.[20]

According to the EEOC's complaint, iTutorGroup's software was configured to automatically reject female applicants aged 55 or older and male applicants aged 60 or older. The discrimination was discovered when an applicant noticed something peculiar. After being rejected for a tutoring position, the applicant decided to conduct an experiment: she submitted a second application that was identical in every way except for one detail—she provided a more recent birth date, making herself appear younger on paper. With the false birth date, she received an interview invitation. With her real age, she was automatically rejected.[21]

The case revealed the peculiar nature of algorithmic discrimination. Unlike implicit bias or prejudice, which can be difficult to prove, iTutorGroup's system embodied explicit, programmed discrimination. Someone at the company had made a deliberate choice to configure the software to categorically exclude applicants based on age and sex. The algorithm was simply executing human prejudice at scale, with perfect consistency.

When the EEOC filed its lawsuit, iTutorGroup initially attempted to defend itself by claiming it was merely a technology provider, not an employer making hiring decisions. But this defense collapsed under scrutiny. The company was hiring tutors to work for its platform—the fact that the hiring process was automated didn't mean iTutorGroup wasn't making employment decisions. The algorithm wasn't a neutral tool; it was an agent of the company's discriminatory intent.

In August 2023, iTutorGroup agreed to settle the case for $365,000, to be distributed among more than 200 rejected applicants. But the monetary compensation was only part of the settlement's significance. More importantly, the company agreed to implement extensive anti-discrimination policies, provide regular training to employees and contractors involved in hiring, invite rejected applicants to reapply, and cease requesting birth dates from applicants during the initial application process. The settlement established a template for holding companies accountable when their AI systems discriminate.[22]

EEOC Chair Charlotte A. Burrows emphasized the significance of the case: "Even when technology automates the discrimination, the employer is still responsible. Workers facing discrimination from an employer's use of technology can count on the EEOC to seek remedies." The message was clear: automation doesn't create a loophole in civil rights law. Companies can't escape accountability by delegating discriminatory decisions to algorithms.

The iTutorGroup case also highlighted a crucial distinction in how algorithmic discrimination occurs. Unlike systems that learn bias from historical data—like the Workday software that Mobley challenged—iTutorGroup's system embodied intentional, programmed discrimination. This raised an important legal question: should we distinguish between algorithms that inadvertently reproduce historical biases and those that are deliberately configured to discriminate?

Some legal scholars argue that intent should matter. When an algorithm is explicitly programmed to exclude protected groups, that's straightforward discrimination under a disparate treatment theory—no different from a human hiring manager who refuses to consider older applicants. But when an algorithm learns to discriminate from biased training data without any explicit instruction to do so, that falls under disparate impact theory, which has different legal standards and defenses.

Yet this distinction may be too neat. Even seemingly neutral algorithms trained on historical data embody human choices about what data to use, how to weight different factors, and what outcomes to optimize for. The University of Washington researchers who found that AI resume screening tools favored white-sounding names 85 percent of the time weren't studying systems explicitly programmed to discriminate. They were examining large language models that had learned associations between race and employability from analyzing patterns in existing hiring data. The bias was learned, not programmed—but it was no less harmful to the people it affected.[23]

The broader challenge is that the myth of algorithmic objectivity makes it easier for organizations to deny responsibility for discriminatory outcomes. When a human hiring manager systematically rejects older applicants, we call it age discrimination. When an algorithm does the same thing, companies often claim it's merely optimizing for some legitimate business criterion that happens to correlate with age. The mathematical veneer makes the discrimination seem somehow more defensible, even when the outcomes are identical.

Toward Meaningful Oversight

The accumulation of algorithmic failures—in hiring, criminal justice, content moderation, and beyond—has sparked a growing movement to establish accountability frameworks for AI systems. These efforts range from voluntary industry standards to binding legal requirements, from technical auditing protocols to institutional oversight mechanisms.

The most ambitious attempt to create a comprehensive accountability regime has come from New York City. In December 2021, after years of debate and advocacy from civil rights groups and technology researchers, the city council passed Local Law 144, the first law in the United States to require independent audits of automated employment decision tools.[24]

The law, which went into effect in July 2023 after further refinements to its implementing rules, requires employers in New York City to conduct annual bias audits of any AI system that substantially assists or replaces discretionary decision-making in hiring or promotions. The audits must test for disparate impact based on race, ethnicity, and sex. The results must be published on the employer's website. Candidates must be notified when AI is being used to evaluate them and must be given information about what data the system analyzes. Violations can result in civil penalties up to $1,500 per violation.[25]

On paper, Local Law 144 seemed like a breakthrough—exactly the kind of transparency and accountability mechanism that advocates had been calling for. In practice, its implementation revealed how difficult it is to create meaningful algorithmic accountability even with legal mandates.

The first challenge was scope. The law applies only to tools that "substantially assist or replace discretionary decision making"—but employers get to decide for themselves whether their systems meet this threshold. Many companies simply determined that their AI tools were not covered by the law, with no mechanism for independent verification.[26]

A study conducted by researchers from Cornell University, Data & Society Research Institute, and Consumer Reports in 2024 found that of 391 large employers in New York City who likely used AI hiring tools, only a tiny fraction had posted bias audits or notices as required by law. The researchers concluded that the law was "falling far short of its goals" and that job seekers could not be expected to find or make use of the disclosures companies were required to make.[27]

The second challenge was the quality and independence of audits. Local Law 144 requires audits to be conducted by "independent" auditors, but it doesn't define what independence means or specify what qualifications auditors should have. The law also doesn't require employers to take any action if an audit reveals bias—only to publish the results.[28]

This created perverse incentives. Companies could shop for friendly auditors who would give them clean bills of health. They could limit audits to narrow technical measures that missed important sources of bias. And crucially, they might be better off not conducting an audit at all—since a published audit showing discrimination could provide evidence for lawsuits—rather than facing the relatively modest penalties for non-compliance.[29]

The third challenge was the limited scope of what the law requires audits to examine. Audits must test for disparate impact based on race, ethnicity, and sex—but not age, disability, or other protected characteristics. They focus on the statistical outputs of algorithms but not on the inputs, training data, or design choices that might introduce bias. And they don't require auditors to assess whether the AI system is actually measuring what it claims to measure—whether it's predicting job performance, as opposed to simply replicating historical patterns of who has been hired in the past.[30]

Despite these limitations, Local Law 144 represented an important milestone. It established the principle that AI systems used to make consequential decisions about people's lives should be subject to independent scrutiny. It created a market for algorithmic auditing services, spurring innovation in auditing methodologies and tools. And it sparked a wave of similar legislation in other jurisdictions, from New Jersey to the European Union, each attempting to improve on New York's model.

Closing the Gap

The accountability gap we face with AI agents is not insurmountable, but closing it will require fundamental changes to how we think about responsibility in algorithmic systems. Based on the failures and partial successes we've examined, several principles for meaningful accountability emerge.

First, accountability must be continuous, not episodic. Traditional accountability mechanisms—annual audits and one-time impact assessments—assume relatively stable systems. But AI agents are dynamic. They learn from new data, adapt to changing environments, and can drift from their original specifications over time. What works on Tuesday might fail on Wednesday. An algorithm that's fair in one context might be discriminatory in another. Meaningful accountability requires continuous monitoring, with mechanisms to detect when systems begin to fail and processes to respond quickly when they do.

Second, accountability must be multi-stakeholder. The people best positioned to identify algorithmic harms are often those experiencing them—job candidates rejected by AI screeners like Derek Mobley, defendants placed on predictive policing lists like Robert McDaniel, and content creators whose work is suppressed by moderation algorithms. Yet accountability frameworks have overwhelmingly been designed around the needs of organizations deploying AI systems, not the people affected by them.

Some promising experiments in participatory oversight point toward alternatives. In Amsterdam, the city government has created a public algorithm register that documents all AI systems used in city services and invites citizen feedback. In Oakland, California, community groups successfully advocated for the creation of a Privacy Advisory Commission with meaningful power to review and reject proposed surveillance technologies, including AI systems. These models suggest that accountability works best when it involves those with lived experience of algorithmic systems, not just technical experts and regulators.

Third, accountability requires transparency, but not just any transparency. Publishing audit results is meaningless if they're written in technical jargon that only specialists can understand. Notifying people that AI is being used to evaluate them is hollow if they have no ability to contest or seek alternatives to algorithmic decision-making. Meaningful transparency means explaining how systems work in ways that are genuinely accessible, providing people with actionable information about how to navigate or challenge algorithmic processes, and creating real channels for redress when systems fail.

Fourth, accountability must have teeth. Voluntary commitments and gentle nudges have repeatedly proven insufficient to change organizational behavior when it comes to AI systems. Companies respond to incentives, and when the costs of implementing robust accountability measures exceed the costs of failing to do so, accountability will remain aspirational. This means enforcement mechanisms with real penalties, private rights of action that allow individuals harmed by algorithms to seek compensation, and industry structures that don't allow companies to externalize the costs of algorithmic failures onto vulnerable populations.

Finally, accountability must grapple with the structural dynamics that make algorithmic harms so persistent. AI agents don't operate in a vacuum. They're embedded in organizations with particular incentives, deployed in markets with specific power dynamics, and shaped by the broader inequalities of the societies in which they function.

Consider again the Workday recruiting system that Mobley challenged. The reason it allegedly discriminates against Black, older, and disabled applicants isn't simply a technical glitch—it's the system working as designed, faithfully reproducing the patterns in employers' existing workforces and hiring histories. Fixing that problem requires more than tweaking the algorithm. It requires confronting the underlying reality that many employers have systematically underrepresented these groups, and that any system trained to replicate "successful" hiring patterns will therefore favor candidates who look like existing employees.

Similarly, the Chicago Strategic Subject List's racial disparities weren't simply a failure of fairness metrics. They reflected deeper realities about how the criminal justice system treats Black and white communities differently—in arrests, charges, police deployment, and surveillance—creating biased data that any predictive algorithm will inherit. Achieving fairness in algorithmic risk assessment isn't just a technical challenge; it requires reckoning with structural racism in the justice system itself.

The Stakes of Accountability

The accountability gap matters not just because it allows individual harms to go unaddressed, though that alone would be reason enough for concern. It matters because accountability is what makes power legitimate in democratic societies. When decisions are made about our lives—who gets hired, who receives credit, who goes to prison, what speech is permitted—we expect to be able to understand those decisions, challenge them when they're wrong, and hold decision-makers responsible when they cause harm.

AI agents are increasingly making these kinds of decisions, but they operate in a space where traditional accountability mechanisms don't easily apply. They're not persons who can be held responsible. They're not fully controlled by any single individual or organization. Their decision-making processes are often opaque even to their creators. And they operate at a scale and speed that makes human oversight difficult even when it's attempted.

This creates a profound threat to the possibility of democratic governance. If more and more consequential decisions are made by systems that no one can fully understand, explain, or control, then power becomes effectively unaccountable. We might still have the forms of democracy—elections, laws, courts—but the substance would hollow out, as the real decisions shaping our lives drift into algorithmic black boxes beyond public scrutiny or control.

The cases examined in this chapter—Workday's allegedly discriminatory recruiting algorithms, Chicago's racially biased Strategic Subject List, iTutorGroup's age-discriminatory screening software, Facebook's catastrophic content moderation failures—reveal not just individual instances of algorithmic failure but a systematic pattern. When AI agents are deployed without robust accountability mechanisms, they tend to reproduce and amplify existing inequalities, operate with minimal transparency, resist external scrutiny, and distribute their harms unevenly, with the most vulnerable populations bearing the greatest burdens.

Yet the same cases also reveal grounds for hope. Derek Mobley's lawsuit against Workday survived multiple motions to dismiss and was certified as a collective action potentially representing hundreds of millions of affected applicants. The Chicago Police Department eventually discontinued its Strategic Subject List after sustained criticism revealed its ineffectiveness and discriminatory impact. iTutorGroup settled with the EEOC and agreed to comprehensive anti-discrimination measures after its programmed age discrimination came to light. New York City's bias audit law, despite its limitations, established a precedent that other jurisdictions are building on.

These partial victories suggest that closing the accountability gap, while difficult, is possible. It requires vigilance from researchers willing to scrutinize black-box algorithms, advocacy from civil rights groups willing to challenge powerful companies and institutions, journalism capable of bringing algorithmic failures to light, and policymakers willing to establish and enforce meaningful standards.

Most importantly, it requires rejecting the framing that algorithmic failures are inevitable—that the complexity and scale of AI systems make accountability impossible. The accountability gap exists not because AI agents are too sophisticated for oversight, but because we have collectively chosen, through countless individual decisions and non-decisions, to deploy powerful systems without adequate safeguards.

The question is not whether we can create accountability for AI agents. It's whether we will. The technologies examined in this chapter are already reshaping hiring, criminal justice, content moderation, and countless other domains. The choice we face is whether these systems will operate as unaccountable mechanisms reproducing existing inequalities, or whether we will insist on building accountability into their design, deployment, and governance from the start.

The chapters that follow explore what meaningful accountability looks like in practice—the institutional frameworks that can provide democratic oversight of AI agents, the design principles that can make AI systems more transparent and contestable, and the strategies individuals and communities can use to maintain agency in an increasingly algorithmic world.

CHAPTER 6

Democratic AI Governance

On July 5, 2023, New York City implemented what many hailed as a landmark achievement in algorithmic accountability. Local Law 144, discussed in the previous chapter, passed after years of advocacy. This law required every employer in the city using automated employment decision tools to conduct independent bias audits and publicly post the results. The law mandated transparency notices to job seekers and gave applicants the right to request a human review instead of algorithmic screening. It was the first legislation of its kind in the world—a bold experiment in democratic oversight of artificial intelligence that other jurisdictions watched closely, eager to learn from America's most populous city.

Within months, it became clear that something had gone terribly wrong.

A team of Cornell University researchers, coordinating 155 student investigators across the city, set out to document compliance with the new law. They visited the websites of 391 major employers—companies that everyone knew used algorithmic hiring tools, from tech giants to retail chains. The results were devastating: only 18 companies had posted the required audit reports. Just 13 had bothered to include transparency notices for job seekers. In a city of eight million people, a groundbreaking accountability law had essentially failed before it began.[1]

C. Shah, *Agent Nation*, https://doi.org/10.1007/979-8-8688-2454-8_6

The problem wasn't simply noncompliance. The researchers discovered something more insidious: a phenomenon they termed "null compliance." Because the law gave companies substantial discretion to determine whether their systems even qualified as automated employment decision tools, investigators couldn't tell if a missing audit meant a company was breaking the law, didn't use such tools, or was simply hiding unfavorable results. The denominator had vanished. Without knowing how many companies should have complied, regulators couldn't calculate a compliance rate. Job seekers couldn't file informed complaints. Researchers couldn't assess algorithmic bias patterns across the city.[2]

Even among the handful of published audits, warning signs emerged. Nearly all reported impact ratios above 0.8—the "four-fifths rule" often used as a threshold in employment discrimination cases—suggesting possible publication bias. Companies were excused from reporting data for demographic groups they hired least, obscuring disparities for the very communities the law aimed to protect. And when audit reports did appear, they were often posted on obscure corners of corporate websites and formatted inconsistently, making them nearly impossible for job seekers to find or understand.

The story of Local Law 144 exposes the central challenge of governing AI agents in democratic societies. Unlike previous waves of automation that replaced clearly defined human tasks, AI agents operate with increasing autonomy across complex, interconnected systems. They make consequential decisions about who gets hired, where police resources deploy, which families receive social services, and how public infrastructure allocates resources. Yet they do so with opacity that defeats traditional accountability mechanisms. When these systems fail or discriminate, responsibility dissipates across a diffuse network of designers, deployers, and vendors. Existing frameworks for corporate and government oversight—built for human decision-makers following explicit rules—struggle to address the distributed, adaptive nature of algorithmic governance.

This chapter confronts that challenge directly. Drawing on successful and failed experiments in algorithmic accountability across multiple jurisdictions, it presents a comprehensive framework for democratic AI governance—institutional structures that can provide meaningful oversight of AI agents without crushing their beneficial capabilities. The path forward requires both learning from the mistakes that doomed Local Law 144 and building on the insights emerging from more successful approaches worldwide.

The Amsterdam Paradox: When Transparency Isn't Enough

While New York City's algorithmic accountability law crumbled under the weight of its own loopholes, Amsterdam took a different approach. In September 2020, the Dutch capital launched one of the world's first algorithm registries—a public database detailing every algorithmic system the city government used to deliver services. Each entry listed the datasets used to train models, described how algorithms were used, explained how humans utilized predictions, and outlined how systems were assessed for bias and risk. Citizens could provide feedback on any algorithm. Contact information for responsible officials was prominently displayed.[3]

The registry was born from Amsterdam's commitment to what Deputy Mayor Touria Meliani proclaimed, "create as much understanding about algorithms as possible." Rather than treating algorithmic systems as proprietary black boxes or relegating oversight to technical experts, the city embraced radical transparency as a foundation for democratic legitimacy. The initiative partnered with Helsinki, Finland, to develop a common data schema that other cities could adopt, establishing standards for algorithmic transparency across Europe. Within months, Barcelona, Bologna, Brussels, Eindhoven, Mannheim, Rotterdam, and Sofia had joined the effort.[4]

Amsterdam seemed to have discovered the formula that had eluded New York: genuine transparency backed by political will. The city wasn't just requiring companies to audit their tools; it was opening its own algorithmic infrastructure to public scrutiny. This approach aligned with the Netherlands' reputation as a global leader in responsible AI governance, ranking first in international indices of AI readiness and accountability.

But transparency alone couldn't overcome the fundamental tension inherent in algorithmic governance. Three years after launching its celebrated registry, Amsterdam found itself at the center of what investigators would call "one of the most devastating case studies in AI ethics history." The city had spent five years and €535,000 developing Smart Check—a welfare fraud detection system meant to prove that AI could be made fair with the right processes and oversight. Amsterdam did everything the AI ethics playbook prescribed: transparent algorithms instead of black boxes, extensive bias testing, community consultation, academic oversight. They published their source code on GitHub for the world to scrutinize.[5]

It still didn't work.

When researchers from Lighthouse Reports and MIT Technology Review conducted the most comprehensive audit of a "responsible AI" system ever undertaken, they uncovered systematic discrimination against residents with migration backgrounds, single mothers, and low-income families—precisely the groups the system was designed to protect. The algorithm assigned risk scores between zero and one based on 15 characteristics from welfare applications. Despite rigorous fairness testing during development, the system replicated and amplified the biases embedded in historical welfare administration.

What made the Smart Check failure particularly illuminating was Amsterdam's extraordinary transparency. Most organizations won't admit that they use algorithms for important decisions, let alone publish detailed documentation. Amsterdam did the opposite. Due to GDPR restrictions, they couldn't simply hand over raw data to investigators, so they created what researchers called a "remote access regime"—running custom analyses on real data and sharing aggregated results. They published multiple versions of the Smart Check algorithm, extensive documentation, bias analysis scripts, and model files. The audit was probably the most transparent algorithmic investigation ever conducted.

That transparency revealed a profound lesson: seeing inside an algorithm isn't the same as governing it democratically. Amsterdam had achieved unprecedented openness about how Smart Check worked. What it hadn't achieved was meaningful public power over whether the system should exist at all, what values should guide its operation, or who should bear the risks of its mistakes. When digital rights advocate Hans de Zwart reviewed the Smart Check documentation, he nearly fell out of his chair—not because the algorithm was opaque, but because no amount of technical optimization could make it acceptable to use an automated system for such consequential determinations of human need.

The Amsterdam paradox crystallizes a crucial insight: democratic AI governance requires more than transparency. It demands structures that give communities genuine power to shape whether and how AI agents operate in domains that affect their lives. Transparency is necessary but not sufficient. Without mechanisms for meaningful public participation in design decisions, algorithmic systems—no matter how well-documented—remain fundamentally technocratic rather than democratic.

Building Algorithms Together: The WeBuildAI Experiment

On a spring evening in 2019, volunteers, donors, recipient organizations, and nonprofit employees gathered in Pittsburgh to design an algorithm. They weren't programmers or data scientists. They were stakeholders in 412 Food Rescue—an on-demand service that matches food donors with volunteers who transport surplus food to organizations serving food-insecure communities. For years, the organization had made these matches manually. Now they wanted an algorithm to help, but they faced a fundamental question: How do you balance efficiency with equity when deciding who gets food?

Should the algorithm prioritize the largest recipient organizations that could handle more food quickly? Or should it ensure smaller community groups receive their fair share? Should it favor volunteers who lived closest to donation sites, minimizing transportation time? Or should it spread opportunities more broadly to engage the community? Should fresh produce go to organizations with commercial kitchens, or to food banks serving families who cook at home? Every technical choice encoded a moral judgment about which values mattered most.[6]

Rather than letting engineers make these decisions unilaterally, the researchers facilitating the project implemented WeBuildAI—a participatory framework that enabled stakeholders to build algorithmic policy for their community. The approach was radically democratic. Each participant created a computational model representing their own beliefs about how the matching algorithm should work. They could choose between machine learning models trained on historical data or explicit rule-based systems that encoded their priorities directly. The framework then aggregated these individual models through a voting process to produce a collective algorithmic policy.

What emerged surprised everyone. Participants successfully built models they felt confident represented their beliefs. The participatory process improved both procedural fairness—stakeholders felt the process was legitimate—and distributive outcomes, producing an algorithm that better balanced competing values than any single expert could have designed. Perhaps most importantly, the exercise raised participants' algorithmic awareness, helping them understand how technical choices shape social outcomes. It also revealed inconsistencies in the nonprofit's own decision-making process that had gone unexamined.

The WeBuildAI experiment demonstrated that community involvement in algorithm design is both feasible and valuable, even for people without technical training. Stakeholders could articulate their values, translate them into computational rules, and collectively negotiate trade-offs. The framework didn't eliminate difficult ethical choices—it made them explicit and subject to democratic deliberation rather than hidden in technical specifications.

Yet the experiment also revealed significant challenges. Creating usable interfaces that allow non-experts to specify algorithmic policies requires substantial design effort. Facilitating meaningful participation demands time and resources that many organizations lack. The framework worked well for a relatively bounded problem with engaged stakeholders who understood the domain. Scaling participatory algorithm design to more complex systems—predictive policing, medical diagnosis, financial credit scoring—poses formidable technical and social challenges.

Still, WeBuildAI offered a glimpse of what democratic AI governance might look like in practice: not experts alone deciding how algorithms should work, but communities actively shaping the systems that govern their lives. The framework treats affected stakeholders as legitimate participants in algorithmic policy-making rather than passive subjects of technical optimization. It recognizes that expertise about domains—who needs food, how communities work, what values matter—belongs to people with lived experience, not just to those who can write code.[7]

Fighting Back: Tenant Advocates Challenge Algorithmic Landlords

When Carmen Arroyo asked her apartment management company in 2016 if her son Mikhail could move in after a bad accident left him unable to care for himself, she expected a straightforward approval process. Instead, an algorithmic tenant screening system called CrimSAFE dredged up a minor shoplifting charge from Mikhail's past—a charge that had no bearing on his ability to be a good tenant or his current circumstances. The request was denied. An algorithm had decided that a years-old, petty offense made Mikhail too risky to live with his mother when he needed her most.[8]

Arroyo could have walked away. Most denied tenants do—they pay another application fee, try another property, and hope the next algorithm treats them better. But Arroyo did something nobody expected: she sued. In 2018, with support from the Connecticut Fair Housing Center and the National Housing Law Project, she filed a federal lawsuit against CoreLogic, the company that produced CrimSAFE. The case argued that tenant screening services are error-prone, result in racial discrimination, and operate largely without accountability. In a historic decision, a federal judge allowed the case to proceed to trial—the first lawsuit of its kind targeting a screening company rather than just a landlord for housing discrimination.

The Arroyo case opened a floodgate. Across America, tenant advocacy groups began recognizing that algorithmic screening tools weren't just making housing decisions faster—they were systematically excluding families from housing opportunities, with disproportionate impacts on Black and Latino renters. The tools swept too broadly, flagging people with dismissed charges, mistaken identities, or old eviction filings that had been resolved. They assigned risk scores without context, treating a decades-old misdemeanor the same as a recent serious offense. And they did so at massive scale, processing millions of applications annually through an industry worth over $1.3 billion.[9]

In Jacksonville, Florida, four residents sued JWB Property Management, alleging that SafeRent Solutions' algorithms disproportionately flagged Black applicants for denial. The plaintiffs had proof that past eviction filings against them had been cleared or dropped, yet the algorithm still marked them as risky. In 2023, Jacksonville Area Legal Aid brought the case to federal court, arguing that AI screening tools were enabling tenant discrimination under the guise of neutral risk assessment. A judge ruled that the case could proceed to trial, forcing SafeRent to defend how its algorithms made decisions.

These lawsuits succeeded where regulatory efforts had stalled. By invoking the Fair Housing Act—a law passed in 1968 to combat racial discrimination in housing—advocates found legal ground to challenge algorithmic bias. The Act's disparate impact doctrine doesn't require proof of intentional discrimination. It's enough to show that a policy or practice, even if facially neutral, has discriminatory effects. Algorithmic screening tools trained on historical data—data poisoned by decades of redlining, employment discrimination, and unequal policing—inevitably perpetuate those inequities. By translating patterns of past discrimination into predictions about future behavior, the algorithms systematize bias at scale.

The tenant advocacy movement forced a reckoning. In May 2024, the Department of Housing and Urban Development issued new guidance requiring human review of tenant screening data to ensure compliance with fair housing laws. The Consumer Financial Protection Bureau fined TransUnion $23 million for inaccurate data in its tenant screening programs. State attorneys general from 15 states sent a joint letter to the Federal Trade Commission demanding scrutiny of tenant screening algorithms. The Justice Department filed an amicus brief in the Arroyo case, arguing that SafeRent's software might violate the Fair Housing Act.[10]

These victories didn't come from top-down regulation or voluntary industry standards. They came from organized communities demanding accountability. Tenant advocacy groups did the painstaking work of documenting how algorithms harmed real people, finding plaintiffs willing to challenge powerful companies and building legal theories that courts would recognize. They succeeded because they understood something fundamental about democratic AI governance: change requires collective action by those most affected by algorithmic systems, not just better design by well-intentioned experts.

The housing algorithm cases offer a template for democratic oversight. When AI agents make consequential decisions about access to fundamental resources—housing, employment, credit, education—affected communities must have standing to challenge those decisions in courts that can provide meaningful remedies. Private companies deploying algorithmic tools must face liability when those tools discriminate, not hide behind claims of trade secrecy or technical complexity. Regulatory agencies must investigate complaints and enforce existing civil rights protections, even when discrimination operates through code rather than explicit human bias.

When Students Said "F**k the Algorithm"

On August 13, 2020, hundreds of thousands of British teenagers woke up to discover their futures had been rewritten by an algorithm. Due to the COVID-19 pandemic, all secondary education examinations that summer had been cancelled. Instead of taking A-level exams—the tests that determine university admission in the UK—students received "calculated grades" generated by a standardization algorithm. The system was designed to combat grade inflation by adjusting teacher predictions based on each school's historical performance over the previous three years.[11]

The results were catastrophic. Nearly 40 percent of students received grades lower than their teachers had predicted—some by multiple grade levels. University offers evaporated. Career plans collapsed. And the algorithm's discrimination was systematic: students from disadvantaged backgrounds saw their grades plummet, while those at small private schools disproportionately received higher calculated grades than their teacher assessments. The algorithm had decided that students' potential should be capped by what other students from their schools had achieved in the past, effectively punishing individuals for attending schools that historically underperformed.[12]

On August 16, hundreds of students gathered in front of the UK Department of Education building in London. They carried signs with a message that would resonate worldwide: "F**k the algorithm." The protest wasn't just about grades. It was about the fundamental injustice of letting an automated system—however sophisticated its mathematics—override teachers' professional judgment about individual students. It was about having your future determined by your school's past performance rather than your own achievements. It was about being treated as a data point in a distribution curve rather than as a person with agency and potential.[13]

The students won. Within days of the protests, facing overwhelming public pressure and threatened legal action, the UK government reversed course entirely. On August 17, education officials announced that all students would receive their teacher-predicted grades instead of the algorithm-generated scores. The head of Ofqual, the regulatory body that developed the algorithm, resigned. So did the most senior civil servant at the Department for Education. Prime Minister Boris Johnson, who had initially defended the results as "robust and dependable," later admitted at a COVID-19 inquiry that he had been in a "homicidal mood" over the scandal.

The A-level debacle exposed something crucial about algorithmic governance: technical sophistication cannot substitute for democratic legitimacy. Ofqual's algorithm was mathematically sound—it achieved its stated objective of maintaining grade distribution patterns similar to previous years. But that objective itself was wrong. By fixating on preventing grade inflation, regulators lost sight of the actual purpose of education assessment: helping students transition to university or employment during anxiety-ridden times. They chose standardization over accuracy, statistical convenience over individual justice.

What made the student protests effective was their immediate recognition that the algorithm wasn't just technically flawed—it was democratically illegitimate. The system made consequential decisions about young people's futures without giving them any meaningful input or appeal. It treated education as a statistical modeling problem rather than a human development process. It subordinated individual potential to aggregate patterns. The students understood intuitively what many AI ethics experts miss: no amount of technical refinement can make fundamentally antidemocratic systems acceptable.

The A-level case also demonstrated the power of what researchers call "critical audiences"—groups of affected people who collectively scrutinize algorithms, challenge their underlying assumptions, and demand accountability. Most algorithmic systems operate without such audiences because their impacts are dispersed, invisible, or hard to attribute to specific technical decisions. The A-level algorithm's impacts were concentrated, visible, and directly felt by hundreds of thousands of students simultaneously. That created conditions for collective mobilization that forced institutional response in days rather than years.

For democratic AI governance, the lesson is clear: affected communities need both the information to understand how algorithms impact them and the power to challenge those impacts when they conflict with democratic values. Transparency without power is voyeurism. Technical expertise without democratic accountability is technocracy. What students demanded—and won—was the right to have important decisions about their futures made by humans who knew them as individuals, not by algorithms that reduced them to statistical inputs.

Toward Democratic AI Governance: Principles and Practices

These stories—from New York's failed law to Amsterdam's transparent failure, from Pittsburgh's participatory success to tenant advocates' legal victories and British students' protests—reveal both the urgency and the difficulty of governing AI agents democratically. They expose why traditional accountability mechanisms fail when confronted with algorithmic systems that learn, adapt, and operate at scales that exceed human oversight capacity. But they also point toward practical frameworks for democratic AI governance that can work.

First, democratic oversight of AI agents must go beyond transparency to include meaningful public participation in design decisions. Amsterdam's algorithm registry succeeded in making information available but failed to give communities power to shape whether and how welfare surveillance systems operated. WeBuildAI showed that even technically complex decisions can be made participatory when stakeholders are given appropriate tools and facilitation. The lesson: transparency is necessary but insufficient. Communities need mechanisms to influence what gets built, not just to see what was built.[14]

Second, effective governance requires clear standards and genuine accountability, not discretion that enables evasion. New York's Local Law 144 failed because it gave companies too much latitude to determine compliance. In contrast, the Fair Housing Act's disparate impact standard gives tenant advocates concrete grounds to challenge discriminatory algorithms through courts that can provide real remedies. Governance frameworks must define what counts as an AI agent subject to oversight, establish measurable standards for fairness and accountability, and create enforcement mechanisms with actual consequences for violations.

Third, democratic AI governance requires diverse stakeholder involvement beyond technical experts. The A-level algorithm failed not because mathematicians made errors, but because they optimized for the wrong objective without input from students, teachers, or education experts who understood what assessment should accomplish. Participatory frameworks must include not just engineers and ethicists but also affected communities, domain experts, and civil society organizations who can identify values and priorities that technical optimization might miss.

Fourth, collective organizing by affected communities remains essential for forcing accountability. Tenant advocacy groups didn't wait for perfect regulations—they used existing civil rights laws creatively to challenge algorithmic discrimination. British students didn't conduct technical audits—they organized protests that made algorithmic injustice politically untenable. Democratic governance emerges from power struggles between those who deploy AI systems and those who live with their consequences, not from voluntary industry commitments to responsibility.

Fifth, governance structures must be adaptive and context-specific. The WeBuildAI framework worked well for a bounded food rescue matching problem with engaged stakeholders. It wouldn't necessarily translate to predictive policing or credit scoring without significant modification. Different domains require different governance approaches: participatory design for community-facing systems, rigorous auditing for high-stakes individual decisions, democratic oversight bodies for infrastructure-level deployments. One-size-fits-all regulations risk being either too restrictive for beneficial applications or too permissive for harmful ones.[15]

What emerges from these principles is not a single governance model but a framework that can be adapted to different contexts while maintaining core democratic values. This framework has several essential components:

- **Algorithmic impact assessments** conducted before deployment that examine not just technical performance but social consequences, with requirements for public comment and stakeholder input. These assessments must be substantive rather than performative, examining whose interests the system serves, what values it embeds, and how it might affect different communities differently.

- **Public algorithm registries** that document what systems operate in public and quasi-public domains, how they work, and who is accountable for them. Unlike Amsterdam's registry, these must include mechanisms for affected communities to challenge systems they find problematic, not just to observe them passively.
- **Participatory design processes** for AI systems that significantly affect communities, using frameworks like WeBuildAI to enable stakeholder input on values and priorities. These processes must be genuinely empowering, not token consultation exercises that provide democratic cover for predetermined technical choices.
- **Independent audit requirements** with clear standards for what constitutes bias, discrimination, or harm. Unlike Local Law 144's toothless requirements, these audits must be conducted by truly independent entities using standardized methodologies, with results published in accessible formats and mechanisms for appeal.
- **Oversight bodies** with diverse membership including affected community representatives, technical experts, domain specialists, and civil rights advocates. These bodies must have actual authority to investigate complaints, compel information disclosure, and recommend or mandate changes to problematic systems.

- **Legal liability frameworks** that enable affected individuals and communities to seek redress when algorithmic systems cause harm. This includes clarifying when AI agents are subject to civil rights protections, establishing standards for algorithmic due process, and ensuring that claims of trade secrecy or technical complexity cannot shield harmful systems from accountability.

These components must work together. Transparency without enforcement is performative. Participation without power is manipulation. Auditing without consequences is theater. Democratic AI governance requires institutional arrangements that make algorithmic systems answerable to the communities they affect, not just to their designers or deployers.

The Stakes of Getting Governance Right

The failures and successes documented in this chapter reveal that we stand at a critical juncture. AI agents are already making consequential decisions about housing, employment, education, criminal justice, and social services. They will soon operate even more autonomously across ever more domains. Whether these systems serve democratic values or undermine them depends on the governance structures we build now, while the technology is still evolving and institutions retain capacity to shape its development.

The technocratic approach that has dominated AI governance—trusting experts to optimize for fairness, safety, and transparency—has proven insufficient. Amsterdam showed that even the most transparent, carefully designed systems can fail to serve democratic values when communities lack power over fundamental design choices. New York demonstrated that regulations without teeth enable evasion rather than accountability. The A-level algorithm illustrated that technical sophistication cannot substitute for democratic legitimacy.

Yet the successes point toward alternatives. Participatory design frameworks like WeBuildAI prove that communities can meaningfully shape algorithmic systems when given appropriate tools and support. Tenant advocacy groups demonstrate that organized communities can use existing legal frameworks to challenge algorithmic discrimination. Student protests show that collective action can force rapid policy reversals when algorithmic injustice becomes politically untenable.

Democratic AI governance is not a technical problem to be solved by better algorithms or more sophisticated auditing tools. It is a socio-political challenge that requires shifting power from those who build and deploy AI systems to those who live with their consequences. This shift demands new institutions, new legal frameworks, and new practices of collective deliberation and decision-making. It requires recognizing that expertise about technical systems is necessary but not sufficient—expertise about domains, communities, and values matters equally.

The alternative to democratic AI governance is not neutrality or purely technical optimization. It is governance by those with the resources to build and deploy algorithmic systems, optimizing for their priorities whether or not those align with broader social welfare. It is AI agents that perpetuate historical inequities because they were trained on data poisoned by past discrimination. It is algorithmic decision-making that fragments communities, concentrates power, and undermines the collective capacity for democratic self-governance.

We can do better. The frameworks outlined in this chapter—participatory design, independent auditing, meaningful transparency, enforceable standards, collective accountability—are not utopian fantasies. They are practical approaches already being implemented in various forms across different jurisdictions. What remains is to scale them up, adapt them to different domains, and embed them in institutions with real authority.

The students who chanted in protest of the algorithm in London understood something fundamental: some decisions are too important to delegate to automated systems, no matter how technically sophisticated. Their protest succeeded because it tapped into a broadly shared intuition that democracy means more than efficient administration—it means preserving human agency and judgment in consequential choices about how we live together. That same insight must guide how we govern the proliferating AI agents that increasingly structure our economic, civic, and personal lives.

The path forward requires both technical innovation and political mobilization. We need better tools for participatory algorithm design, more sophisticated approaches to algorithmic auditing, and clearer standards for measuring bias and discrimination. But we also need organized communities demanding accountability, legal frameworks enabling challenges to algorithmic harm, and political institutions willing to constrain algorithmic systems that serve narrow interests rather than broad public welfare.

Democratic AI governance is possible. This chapter has shown how it can work in practice, what obstacles it faces, and what principles should guide its implementation. Whether we achieve it depends not on technological breakthroughs but on political will—the willingness of communities to demand meaningful power over the algorithmic systems that shape their lives, and the willingness of institutions to grant that power even when it complicates technical optimization.

CHAPTER 7

Designing Human-Centered AI Agents

The conference room in Amazon's Seattle headquarters hummed with the quiet confidence of technological inevitability. It was 2014, and a team of machine learning engineers had gathered to unveil what they called their "holy grail"—an AI system that would revolutionize how the world's largest e-commerce company found talent. The pitch was elegant in its simplicity: feed the algorithm a hundred resumes, and it would instantly identify the top five candidates. No more endless hours of human review. No more subjective biases clouding judgment. Just pure, data-driven meritocracy.

"Everyone wanted this," one engineer would later recall, their voice thick with the memory of what came next. "They literally wanted it to be an engine where I'm going to give you 100 resumes, it will spit out the top five, and we'll hire those."[1]

By 2015, the dream had curdled into a nightmare. The AI, trained on a decade of resumes submitted to Amazon—overwhelmingly from men in a male-dominated industry—had taught itself a sinister lesson: male candidates were preferable. It penalized resumes containing the word "women's," as in "women's chess club captain." It downgraded graduates of two all-women's colleges. When engineers tried to scrub these specific biases from the code, they discovered something more troubling: they couldn't guarantee the machine wouldn't find other, subtler ways to discriminate.[2]

C. Shah, *Agent Nation*, https://doi.org/10.1007/979-8-8688-2454-8_7

By early 2017, Amazon had quietly disbanded the team. The holy grail remained out of reach.

But here's what makes this story more than just another cautionary tale about AI gone wrong: Amazon's failure contained the seeds of a different future. Because while Amazon's engineers were discovering what *not* to do, technologists and organizations around the world were learning how to design AI agents that genuinely serve human flourishing. The question wasn't whether AI agents would reshape hiring, healthcare, and countless other domains—that ship had already sailed. The question was whether those agents would be designed with human values at their core, or whether they would simply automate and amplify our worst instincts at digital speed.

This chapter is about that choice, and about the people and organizations making it differently.

The Anatomy of Failure

To understand how to build AI agents that enhance rather than undermine human autonomy, we first need to understand why they fail. Amazon's recruiting algorithm wasn't broken in some superficial way that could be fixed with a software patch. The problem ran deeper, to the very core of how the system learned to see the world.

The engineers had made what seemed like a reasonable choice: train the AI on historical data—ten years of resumes from people Amazon had actually hired. The machine would study these examples and learn to recognize the patterns of success. That seems like a reasonable idea; after all, humans do the same. Don't they? Perhaps, but that doesn't make it so right. Historical data is never neutral. It's a fossil record of past decisions, complete with all the biases, assumptions, and structural inequalities those decisions embodied.

In Amazon's case, that fossil record showed a stark reality: the company's technical workforce was overwhelmingly male. Not because men were inherently better engineers, but because of decades of systemic barriers that had kept women out of computer science programs, discriminated against them in hiring, and driven them out of tech careers through hostile work environments. The AI, with its cold efficiency, simply learned to replicate these patterns. It wasn't making moral judgments about gender. It was making statistical inferences about what Amazon had valued in the past.

The deeper problem lay in how success had been defined. The algorithm's creators had assumed that past hiring decisions represented some kind of ground truth about candidate quality. But hiring decisions are themselves judgments made by humans with biases, working within systems shaped by inequality. By training the AI to reproduce these decisions, Amazon's engineers had created a sophisticated machine for perpetuating discrimination at scale.

P.K. Kannan, Dean's Chair in Marketing Science at the University of Maryland's Robert H. Smith School of Business, explained the compounding nature of the problem: "With machine learning, if an algorithm is used day in and day out, the mistake builds up."[3] Small errors in the training data don't just persist—they multiply. If the AI's biased recommendations were fed back into the next generation of training data, the system would become progressively more discriminatory over time.

This feedback loop represents one of the fundamental challenges in designing human-centered AI agents: how do we break free from the gravity of the past? How do we build systems that learn from historical data without being imprisoned by it?

The Path to Redemption: Unilever's Transformation

While Amazon was quietly shelving its failed experiment, another global giant was embarking on a radically different approach to AI-powered recruitment. Unilever, the consumer goods conglomerate behind everything from Dove soap to Ben & Jerry's ice cream, faced a daunting challenge: processing 1.8 million job applications annually while hiring more than 30,000 employees across the globe. The traditional approach—resume screening followed by multiple rounds of interviews—was expensive, time-consuming, and, research suggested, riddled with human bias.

But Unilever's approach to AI recruitment diverged from Amazon's in a crucial way. Rather than simply automating existing processes, they redesigned the entire system from the ground up, centering human values at every stage.

The transformation began with a fundamental question: What if we stopped asking AI to judge candidates based on their resumes? Resumes, after all, often say more about privilege and access than about actual ability. Someone who attended an elite university may have had opportunities that others never did. Someone whose resume shows job-hopping might have been dealing with family obligations or working multiple jobs to make ends meet. The resume is a proxy measure, and not always a good one.

Instead, Unilever partnered with companies like Pymetrics and HireVue to create a multi-stage assessment process that evaluated cognitive abilities, emotional intelligence, and job-specific skills through gamified tests and AI-analyzed video interviews. Crucially, these tools were designed with human oversight and iterative feedback built in. AI would provide initial assessments, but human recruiters would review recommendations, especially in cases where the AI showed uncertainty.

The company also established protocols for regularly auditing the system for bias, examining whether it produced equitable outcomes across different demographic groups.[4]

The results were striking. Unilever reduced its hiring time by 75 percent—from four months to just a few weeks. More importantly, the diversity of its candidate pool increased by 16 percent. By 2021, the company was hiring thousands of people a year without using a single resume.[5]

But raw numbers don't capture the full picture. What made Unilever's approach successful wasn't just the technology—it was the intentional design choices behind it. The company had moved beyond thinking of AI as a tool for optimizing existing processes and instead asked: What if we designed a hiring system around the values we actually wanted to embody?

This shift from optimization to values-based design represents a fundamental paradigm change in how organizations approach AI development. Traditional software engineering focuses on defining clear objectives and then building systems to achieve them as efficiently as possible. But with AI agents operating in complex social contexts, efficiency in achieving narrow objectives can come at the cost of broader human values. Unilever succeeded not because its AI was more sophisticated than Amazon's, but because the company approached the problem with a different set of questions: What outcomes do we actually want? Who might be harmed by this system? How can we design for equity from the beginning?

The company established governance structures to continually evaluate the AI's performance, not just in terms of hiring speed or cost savings, but in terms of fairness and candidate experience. They measured whether candidates felt the process was respectful and transparent. They tracked outcomes across different demographic groups to catch emerging biases before they became entrenched. They maintained human judgment in the loop, especially for complex or high-stakes decisions.

This is what human-centered AI design looks like in practice: not as a one-time technical fix, but as an ongoing commitment to align technology with human values.

Healthcare's Collaborative Intelligence

If the hiring failures of Amazon and the successes of Unilever teach us about the importance of values-based design in algorithmic decision-making, healthcare offers an even more profound lesson: sometimes the most powerful AI agents are those explicitly designed to *enhance* rather than replace human judgment.

The case of acute respiratory distress syndrome (ARDS) detection provides a compelling example. ARDS is a life-threatening condition where the lungs become severely inflamed and fail to provide adequate oxygen to the bloodstream. It's notoriously difficult to diagnose from chest X-rays alone—even experienced radiologists disagree about 25 percent of the time. The condition requires rapid treatment, but misdiagnosis can lead to inappropriate interventions that harm rather than help.

Researchers developed an AI model capable of detecting ARDS patterns on chest X-rays with accuracy matching or exceeding individual physicians. But rather than simply deploying the AI to replace human doctors, they took a different approach. They tested four different collaboration strategies to find which combination of AI and physician judgment produced the best outcomes.[6]

The winning strategy wasn't AI replacing doctors, nor doctors overriding AI whenever they disagreed. Instead, it was a carefully choreographed dance: the AI reviewed images first and made its assessment. In cases where the AI was confident, it made a recommendation. But when the AI detected uncertainty—when the images showed patterns it hadn't seen in training, or when the diagnosis was genuinely ambiguous—it deferred to the physician. This human-AI collaboration achieved higher diagnostic accuracy than either AI or physicians working alone.

The implications extend far beyond ARDS diagnosis. This research revealed something crucial about how to design AI agents for high-stakes domains: the goal isn't to remove humans from the loop, but to create systems where human expertise and machine capabilities complement each other. The AI brings speed, consistency, and the ability to detect subtle patterns across millions of cases. Humans bring contextual understanding, the ability to integrate information from multiple sources, and most crucially, the capacity for moral judgment and empathy.

A more recent study examining how physicians interact with GPT-4 in chest pain triage scenarios found that doctors were willing to modify their clinical decisions based on AI recommendations, leading to improved diagnostic accuracy. Most significantly, the AI assistance didn't introduce or exacerbate demographic biases—accuracy improvements were consistent across white male and Black female patients.[7]

But the study also revealed something more nuanced. Physicians didn't blindly follow AI recommendations. They evaluated them against their own clinical knowledge, their understanding of the specific patient, and their sense of what made medical sense. The AI was most helpful when physicians understood its capabilities and limitations—when it was positioned not as an oracle but as a knowledgeable colleague whose opinion should be considered alongside other sources of information.

This collaborative model challenges the prevailing narrative that AI will inevitably replace human workers. Instead, it suggests a different future: one where AI agents are explicitly designed to amplify human capabilities rather than supplant them. But this future doesn't happen automatically. It requires intentional design choices at every level.

The Architecture of Human-Centered Design

What separates Amazon's failure from Unilever's success? What enabled healthcare AI to enhance rather than replace physician judgment? The answer lies not in the sophistication of the algorithms, but in the frameworks and processes used to design and deploy them.

Over the past decade, a constellation of researchers, practitioners, and standards organizations have been developing methodologies for embedding human values into AI systems from the ground up. Perhaps the most comprehensive of these efforts is IEEE 7000, a standard published in 2021 that provides organizations with a step-by-step process for addressing ethical concerns throughout the system design lifecycle.[88]

IEEE 7000 emerged from five years of work by 154 experts spanning multiple disciplines—engineers, philosophers, theologians, ethicists—and representing diverse cultural perspectives from Europe, the Middle East, the Americas, Asia, and Africa. The standard's foundational insight is deceptively simple: ethical concerns can't be bolted onto technology as an afterthought. They must be woven into the design process from the beginning.

The standard guides organizations through a values-based engineering process. It starts with a crucial question: Who are the stakeholders affected by this system, and what do they value? Not what do *we* think they *should* value, but what do *they* actually care about? This seemingly straightforward question often reveals surprising complexity. The stakeholders in a hiring AI, for example, include not just the company and the candidates who apply, but also current employees whose work environment might be affected, customers who care about corporate values, and broader communities impacted by employment patterns.

Once stakeholders and their values have been identified, IEEE 7000 provides methods for translating those values into concrete system requirements. If fairness is a key value, what does fairness mean in this specific context? Equal representation across demographic groups? Equal opportunity despite differing backgrounds? Equal outcomes? Different stakeholders may have different—and sometimes conflicting—notions of fairness, and part of the design process involves making those tensions explicit and deciding how to navigate them.

The standard also requires ongoing monitoring and evaluation. Once an AI agent is deployed, how will the organization know if it's actually serving the values it was designed to uphold? What metrics will be tracked? Who will review the data? What mechanisms exist for identifying and correcting problems? These questions must be answered during design, not discovered in crisis.

Sarah Spiekermann, Vice-Chair of IEEE 7000 and Chair of the Institute for Information Systems & Society at Vienna University of Economics and Business, notes that organizations applying the standard typically identify ten potential ethical issues per person involved in the project.[9] This isn't because the process creates problems that weren't there before—it's because it makes visible the ethical dimensions of technical choices that often go unexamined.

The IEEE 7000 family has since expanded to encompass multiple related standards: P7001 on transparency of autonomous systems, P7003 on algorithmic bias, P7005 on employer data governance, and others. Together, they represent an emerging infrastructure for responsible AI development.

But standards alone aren't enough. They need to be embedded in organizational culture and supported by practical tools and methodologies.

The Open-Source Alternative

While traditional software companies like Amazon struggled with black-box AI systems that even their creators couldn't fully explain, a different model was emerging from the open-source community. Hugging Face, a company built around democratizing access to machine learning, was demonstrating how transparency and community involvement could create better AI agents while maintaining both innovation and commercial viability.

Founded in 2016, Hugging Face began as a chatbot company but evolved into something far more significant: a platform where anyone could share, discover, and collaborate on AI models and datasets. By 2024, the platform hosted over 350,000 machine learning models contributed by researchers, engineers, and organizations worldwide. But what makes Hugging Face distinctive isn't just the scale of its repository—it is the ethical framework woven into the platform's design.[10]

At the heart of Hugging Face's approach are *model cards*—standardized documentation that accompanies each AI model on the platform. These aren't technical specifications buried in academic papers. They're accessible documents that explain what the model does, what data it was trained on, what its limitations are, and what ethical considerations users should be aware of. If a model was trained predominantly on English-language text from Internet sources, the model card makes that clear, along with the implications for non-English speakers or for topics underrepresented online. The model cards are inspired by nutritional labels that we see in most packaged food products sold in grocery stores. They are standardized, regulated, and you don't have to be a food safety expert or a dietitian to interpret them.

This commitment to transparency extends to tools for detecting and measuring bias. Hugging Face developed evaluation frameworks that allow developers to test their models across different demographic groups and identify disparate impacts before deployment. When the company released its own multimodal model, IDEFICS, in 2023, it publicly shared the results of bias and harm testing, documenting where the model performed well and where it struggled.[11]

But perhaps most significantly, Hugging Face has created mechanisms for community accountability. Any user can flag problematic models or datasets, opening a discussion in the repository's community tab. Rather than having a central authority make unilateral decisions about what's acceptable, the platform creates spaces for affected communities to voice concerns and for developers to respond. It's a form of distributed governance that acknowledges different perspectives and values while maintaining community standards.

This isn't just idealism—it's proved commercially successful. By building trust through transparency, Hugging Face has attracted partnerships with major tech companies, research institutions, and government agencies. Organizations use Hugging Face's tools precisely because they provide visibility into how AI models work and what their limitations are. In regulated industries like healthcare and finance, where algorithmic decisions must be auditable and explainable, this transparency is essential.

The company's Chief Ethics Scientist, Margaret Mitchell, and her colleagues have also engaged directly with policymakers, providing technical input on regulations like the European Union's AI Act. By bringing open-source values into policy discussions, they've helped shape frameworks that balance innovation with accountability.[12]

What the Hugging Face model demonstrates is that transparency and commercial success aren't incompatible. In fact, in an era where algorithmic failures can destroy reputation and trigger regulatory action, transparency becomes a competitive advantage. Companies that can demonstrate their AI systems are well-documented, regularly audited for bias, and responsive to community concerns build trust that purely proprietary "black-box" approaches cannot match.

The Oversight Problem: Meta's Experiment

If Unilever represents successful values-based design in corporate AI deployment, and Hugging Face demonstrates the power of open-source transparency, Meta's Oversight Board offers a different case study: an attempt to create external accountability for AI-driven content moderation at planetary scale.

In November 2018, after years of criticism over how Facebook handled harmful content, CEO Mark Zuckerberg announced plans for an independent body that could override the company's content moderation decisions. He described it as a kind of "Supreme Court" for Facebook, giving it quasi-judicial authority to review controversial cases and set precedents.[13]

The Oversight Board officially began work in October 2020 with 20 members—academics, lawyers, human rights activists, a former Danish prime minister, and others from around the world. The board's mandate was ambitious: review appeals from users whose content had been removed, make binding decisions on specific cases, and issue policy recommendations to Meta. The company committed to implementing the board's case decisions and responding to policy recommendations within 60 days.

By 2024, the board had reviewed over 100 cases and overturned Meta's original decisions in roughly 80 percent of them. This high overturn rate suggested that Meta's internal moderation systems—increasingly automated through AI—were making questionable calls.[14]

But the board's actual impact remained limited by a fundamental constraint: it couldn't review or mandate changes to Meta's recommendation algorithms, advertising systems, or the AI models that made the overwhelming majority of content moderation decisions. It could only rule on individual pieces of content after someone appealed. Meanwhile, Meta's AI systems were making millions of automated moderation decisions daily—removing posts, demoting content, or restricting accounts based on algorithmic judgments that operated largely beyond the board's purview.[15]

The Oversight Board highlighted a crucial challenge in AI agent governance: how do you create meaningful accountability for systems that operate at a scale and speed that exceed human capacity for review? Meta's content moderation AI processes millions of images, videos, and text posts every day. The Oversight Board might review 30 cases annually. It was like trying to steer an ocean liner with a canoe paddle.

The board's members recognized this limitation and pushed for greater access to Meta's algorithmic systems. In their 2023 annual report, they called for transparency into how the company's AI models made decisions, what training data they used, and how often they produced errors across different communities and contexts. They argued that without understanding the algorithmic infrastructure making the majority of moderation decisions, they couldn't fulfill their oversight role effectively.

Meta's response was revealing. The company provided some additional data and access, but resisted giving the board full transparency into its core algorithmic systems, citing competitive concerns and the complexity of modern AI models. This tension between proprietary technology and public accountability remains unresolved—not just at Meta, but across the AI industry.

The Oversight Board experiment teaches several lessons about AI agent governance. First, external oversight mechanisms must have teeth—they need access to the systems they're meant to oversee, not just to their outputs. Second, case-by-case review doesn't scale to match the pace of AI decision-making; oversight needs to focus on the systems and processes that generate decisions, not just individual decisions themselves. Third, meaningful accountability requires that companies document their AI systems' design, training, and performance in ways that external evaluators can understand and audit.

Despite its limitations, the Oversight Board represented a significant evolution in thinking about AI governance. It acknowledged that the companies deploying powerful AI agents have obligations beyond maximizing user engagement or shareholder value. It created a precedent for independent oversight and public deliberation about content moderation decisions. And it revealed the tensions between commercial interests, technological complexity, and public accountability that any governance framework must navigate.

From Theory to Practice: Education and Professional Standards

Understanding the principles of human-centered AI design is one thing. Creating a generation of practitioners who can implement those principles is another. Over the past decade, universities and professional organizations have begun transforming how they train the next generation of AI developers.

Carnegie Mellon University, one of the world's leading AI research centers, redesigned its computer science curriculum to integrate ethics throughout, rather than relegating it to a single elective course. Students now encounter ethical considerations in their algorithms courses, their machine learning classes, and their capstone projects. When they learn about optimization techniques, they also learn about value alignment—how to ensure the values being optimized actually match human goals. When they study neural networks, they study fairness metrics and bias detection.

This integration reflects a crucial insight: ethics isn't a separate topic from technical AI development. Every technical choice has ethical implications. The decision about what training data to use, which optimization objective to maximize, how to handle uncertain predictions—these are simultaneously technical and ethical questions.

Separating them creates graduates who can build sophisticated AI systems but lack the frameworks to ask whether those systems should be built, or how they might be designed differently to better serve human flourishing.

Professional organizations have also moved toward establishing standards for AI practitioners. In July 2018, the Association for Computing Machinery (ACM) updated its Code of Ethics to explicitly address AI and algorithmic accountability. The code now requires that computing professionals ensure that systems they design "minimize negative consequences to health, safety, personal security, and privacy" and that they "recognize and take special care of systems that become integrated into the infrastructure of society."[16]

The IEEE, through its Global Initiative on Ethics of Autonomous and Intelligent Systems, has gone further, creating not just standards but an entire ecosystem of resources for practitioners. Their "Ethically Aligned Design" framework provides specific guidance for engineers at different career stages, from students first learning to code to senior architects designing enterprise AI systems. The framework emphasizes that ethical AI development requires interdisciplinary collaboration—bringing together not just different kinds of engineers, but ethicists, social scientists, affected communities, and domain experts.

These educational and professional initiatives matter because they shape the assumptions and instincts that practitioners bring to their work. An engineer who has spent four years learning that algorithmic bias is a technical problem to be solved will approach AI design differently than one who has never encountered the concept. A manager who understands the importance of diverse perspectives in AI development will build different teams than one focused solely on technical credentials.

The Economics of Ethical AI

A persistent myth in AI development is that ethical design costs too much—that companies choosing values-based approaches will be outcompeted by those focused purely on technical performance and speed to market. The stories of Unilever, Hugging Face, and others suggest otherwise.

Unilever's ethical AI recruitment system saved the company money even as it improved fairness. By reducing time-to-hire by 75 percent, the company freed up significant human resources for higher-value activities. The improved candidate experience strengthened Unilever's employer brand, making it easier to attract top talent. And by increasing diversity, the company gained documented benefits in creativity, problem-solving, and market understanding that homogeneous teams lack.

Similarly, Hugging Face's commitment to transparency and open-source values hasn't prevented it from building a successful business. By 2024, the company had raised hundreds of millions in funding and counted major tech companies, research institutions, and government agencies among its customers. Organizations chose Hugging Face precisely because its values-based approach provided the documentation, auditability, and community oversight that regulated industries require.

The economic case for human-centered AI rests on several factors. First, avoiding costly failures: Amazon's abandoned recruiting tool represented millions in wasted investment. Companies that catch bias and other problems during design rather than after deployment save money and reputation. Second, meeting regulatory requirements: as governments worldwide establish AI regulations, companies with documented ethics processes and transparent systems will have advantages over those scrambling to retrofit accountability. Third, building trust: in an era where algorithmic failures make headlines and erode public confidence, demonstrating genuine commitment to ethical AI becomes a competitive differentiator.

But perhaps most fundamentally, the economic argument for ethical AI recognizes that optimization of narrow metrics often destroys broader value. An algorithm that maximizes short-term engagement by recommending increasingly extreme content might boost advertising revenue temporarily, but at the cost of user wellbeing, democratic discourse, and ultimately the platform's sustainability. An AI agent that cuts hiring time by simply filtering out qualified candidates who don't fit historical patterns might improve process efficiency while harming the organization's ability to innovate and adapt.

Human-centered AI design asks: What are we really trying to achieve? And are the metrics we're optimizing actually proxies for those deeper goals? This questioning often reveals opportunities for value creation that purely technical optimization would miss.

The Implementation Challenge

Understanding human-centered design principles doesn't automatically translate to implementing them in organizations facing pressure for rapid deployment and competitive markets. The gap between knowing what should be done and actually doing it represents one of the central challenges in ethical AI development.

Consider the practical obstacles facing a product team tasked with developing an AI agent:

- **Time pressure:** Executives want to see results quickly. Competitors are moving fast. Taking time to carefully consider stakeholder values, identify potential harms, and design appropriate safeguards can feel like a luxury the company can't afford.

- **Complexity:** Modern AI systems involve multiple teams, third-party tools, and legacy systems. Implementing human-centered design across this ecosystem requires coordination and buy-in from many stakeholders, each with their own priorities and constraints.

- **Uncertainty:** Unlike traditional engineering problems with clear specifications, human-centered AI design involves navigating competing values and making judgment calls about which trade-offs are acceptable. Engineers trained to seek optimal solutions may struggle with problems where "optimal" is contextual and contested.
- **Measurement difficulty:** It's easy to measure system accuracy or processing speed. It's much harder to measure fairness, transparency, or alignment with human values. What gets measured gets managed, and without good metrics for human-centered outcomes, they tend to get deprioritized.

Successful implementation requires addressing these obstacles systematically. Organizations that have made progress share several characteristics:

- **Leadership commitment:** Human-centered AI design can't be delegated to a single "ethics team" while the rest of the organization operates under different principles. It requires leaders who understand the stakes and are willing to invest resources and accept some friction in the pursuit of better outcomes.
- **Clear governance structures:** Who has authority to raise concerns about potential harms? What happens when values conflict with business metrics? How are

trade-offs decided, and by whom? Without answers to these questions, good intentions dissolve into confusion when real decisions must be made.

- **Interdisciplinary collaboration:** Technical teams need access to expertise in ethics, social science, law, and domain-specific knowledge. Organizations that create formal mechanisms for interdisciplinary collaboration—standing committees, required consultations, embedded ethicists—see better outcomes than those that treat ethics as an optional add-on.
- **Incentive alignment**: If engineers and managers are evaluated solely on technical performance metrics, they'll optimize for those metrics even when doing so creates ethical problems. Evaluation systems need to incorporate human-centered outcomes alongside traditional technical measures.

The healthcare collaborations between AI systems and physicians demonstrate what effective implementation can look like. Researchers didn't just develop algorithms and hand them to hospitals. They worked with clinicians to understand their workflows, their information needs, and their trust-building processes. They tested different human-AI collaboration strategies to find which worked best in practice. They created interfaces that made AI recommendations transparent and contestable. And they measured success not just by diagnostic accuracy but by physician trust, patient outcomes, and whether the systems were actually used in clinical practice.

This iterative, collaborative, human-centered approach to implementation takes longer than simply deploying an algorithm and hoping for the best. But it produces systems that actually work in the messy reality of human organizations and social contexts.

Building an AI Ethics Culture: Education and Professional Standards

While frameworks like IEEE 7000 provide crucial technical scaffolding for ethical AI development, lasting change requires transforming how we educate and train the next generation of AI practitioners. A 2025 systematic review of AI ethics education found that while 86 percent of universities report awareness of AI regulations, fewer than 25 percent have fully implemented comprehensive governance programs.[17] The gap between policy development and operational implementation remains vast.

California State University, Fullerton took a different approach. In early 2025, a multidisciplinary team led by Professor Shelli Wynants developed the ETHICAL Principles AI Framework for Higher Education—a comprehensive model designed to provide flexible, adaptable guidance for responsible AI use across diverse academic contexts.[18] Rather than imposing rigid rules, the framework emphasizes seven interconnected principles: Equity, Transparency, Human Oversight, Integrity, Collaboration, Accountability, and Learning.

What distinguished this approach was its recognition that AI ethics cannot be taught as a separate module tacked onto technical training. Instead, the framework called for integrating ethical considerations throughout curriculum design, from introductory programming courses to advanced machine learning seminars. Students don't just learn *how* to build AI systems; they learn to ask fundamental questions about *why* those systems should exist and *whom* they should serve.

The framework's impact extended beyond classroom instruction. Faculty development programs helped educators cultivate what researchers call "ethical attitudes and behaviors" in AI use—moving beyond compliance checklists to develop genuine ethical reflexivity.[19] This matters because technical competence without ethical grounding can produce precisely the kind of systems that Amazon's recruiting algorithm exemplified: technically sophisticated but fundamentally flawed.

Similar initiatives emerged across higher education. Miami University established interdisciplinary AI ethics committees that brought together computer scientists, philosophers, social scientists, and affected community representatives.[20] These committees didn't just review research protocols; they actively shaped how AI systems were conceived and deployed across campus operations, from admissions algorithms to learning management systems.

Professional organizations also stepped up. Beyond IEEE's formal standards, the Association for Computing Machinery (ACM) updated its Code of Ethics in 2018 to explicitly address AI systems, establishing clear expectations that computing professionals should "contribute to society and to human wellbeing, acknowledging that all people are stakeholders in computing."[21] This wasn't aspirational language—it created professional accountability mechanisms in which failing to consider stakeholder values constitutes a violation of professional standards.

The educational transformation goes beyond universities. Corporate training programs increasingly recognize that technical skills alone don't produce ethical AI. By 2025, 87 percent of business leaders reported plans to implement AI ethics policies, though actual implementation lagged significantly.[22] The gap between intention and action revealed a crucial insight: ethics education must be ongoing, practical, and embedded in daily work—not a one-time training module that employees click through to satisfy compliance requirements.

Participatory AI Design: Giving Communities Real Power

While education builds ethical capacity, participatory design ensures that AI systems actually reflect the values and needs of affected communities. Traditional AI development often treats users as data sources or test subjects. Participatory approaches flip this dynamic, giving communities genuine power to shape how AI systems operate in domains that affect their lives.

Barcelona's experience with the Decidim platform demonstrates what's possible when participation moves beyond consultation to genuine co-design. Launched in 2016, Decidim created an open-source digital platform that allows residents to directly influence policy decisions about urban planning, resource allocation, and municipal services.[23] By 2024, over 400 municipalities worldwide had adopted the platform, processing more than 40,000 participatory proposals and enabling millions of citizens to shape algorithmic governance of their cities.

What made Decidim transformative wasn't just the technology—it was the commitment to radical transparency and democratic legitimacy. Every algorithmic decision about how proposals are surfaced, discussed, and prioritized is documented and open to public scrutiny. Citizens don't just use the system; they can examine its code, propose modifications, and vote on how it should evolve. This transparency builds trust while creating accountability mechanisms absent from proprietary AI systems.

In the United States, San Antonio took a different but equally participatory approach with its Smart City Sandboxes initiative. Rather than deploying AI systems and hoping residents would adapt, the city created interactive spaces where citizens could experiment with proposed technologies, provide feedback, and help shape implementation priorities.[24] The sandboxes became laboratories for democratic AI governance, revealing community concerns that technical experts had overlooked and surfacing use cases that bureaucratic planning processes had missed.

Perhaps most innovative was the approach developed by researchers working with the Alaska Tribal Health System. Recognizing that AI systems trained on data from predominantly white populations could perpetuate health disparities for Alaska's Native communities, they developed a Community-Engaged Artificial Intelligence framework that put indigenous communities at the center of AI design from the beginning.[25]

The framework emphasized what researchers called "upstream" participation—involving communities not just in testing or feedback, but in determining whether AI systems should exist at all, what problems they should address, and whose knowledge should inform their development. This approach acknowledged that technical efficiency matters far less than cultural appropriateness and community trust. An AI system that technically "works" but violates cultural values or erodes community autonomy isn't successful—it's harmful.

These participatory approaches share crucial characteristics: they treat affected communities as genuine experts whose knowledge is essential, not optional; they build in mechanisms for ongoing governance rather than one-time consultation; and they recognize that technical decisions are inherently political, shaping power relations and resource distribution in ways that demand democratic oversight.

The challenge remains in scaling these approaches. Participatory design is more time-consuming and complex than traditional top-down development. It requires humility from technical experts, patience from all stakeholders, and institutional structures that can accommodate genuine power-sharing. But the alternative—AI systems imposed on communities without their input or consent—has proven both ethically problematic and practically ineffective.

Corporate Governance: Making Ethics Operational

Individual ethics and participatory processes matter, but they require institutional structures that can translate principles into practice. Corporate governance mechanisms—from ethics boards to audit procedures—determine whether human-centered AI remains an aspiration or becomes operational reality.

Novartis, the Swiss pharmaceutical giant, offers a compelling model. In 2023, the company's CEO-chaired Environmental, Social, and Governance (ESG) committee approved a comprehensive AI framework ensuring that ethical considerations became integral to top-level strategic decisions.[26] This wasn't a separate ethics review process bolted onto existing operations; it embedded AI governance into the highest levels of corporate decision-making.

"The responsible use of AI requires both clear ethical commitments and a comprehensive risk and compliance framework," explained Klaus Moosmayer, Novartis's Chief Ethics, Risk, and Compliance Officer.[27] The company didn't just develop policies—it created accountability structures ensuring that AI systems couldn't be deployed without demonstrating alignment with ethical principles.

The approach reflected broader trends in corporate AI governance. By early 2025, the percentage of S&P 500 companies disclosing some form of AI board oversight had increased by more than 84 percent year-over-year, with 31 percent reporting specific committee oversight responsibility, directors with AI expertise, or dedicated AI ethics boards.[28] Audit committees emerged as the primary choice for AI oversight, though the specifics varied significantly across companies.

However, disclosure doesn't equal effectiveness. While 73 percent of C-suite executives believe ethical AI guidelines are important, only 6 percent had actually developed them as of late 2024.[29] This implementation gap reveals a crucial challenge: creating governance structures requires not just good intentions but genuine organizational change, including budget allocation, staff expertise, and willingness to slow down or halt AI deployments when problems emerge.

Effective corporate governance also requires external accountability. Investor pressure has proven surprisingly influential. Norway's $1.4 trillion sovereign wealth fund developed its own standards for companies it invests in, setting clear expectations for responsible and ethical AI use.[30] When one of the world's largest institutional investors demands AI ethics as a condition of investment, companies pay attention—not just to reputational concerns but to material financial implications.

Shareholder proposals on AI governance quadrupled from 2023 to 2024, with investors demanding transparency about algorithmic bias, clear oversight responsibilities, and measurable outcomes.[31] This shift reflected growing recognition that AI ethics isn't just a social responsibility issue—it's a smart long-term investment strategy. Companies that fail to govern AI systems responsibly face regulatory penalties, reputational damage, litigation risk, and loss of consumer trust.

These governance mechanisms work best when they're integrated rather than isolated. Education builds ethical capacity in individuals. Participatory processes ensure community voices shape development. Professional standards create peer accountability. Corporate governance translates all of this into operational practice. And external oversight—from investors, regulators, and civil society—provides the enforcement mechanisms that make governance meaningful rather than performative.

The Road Ahead

The stories in this chapter—Amazon's failure and Unilever's success, healthcare's collaborative intelligence and Meta's oversight experiments, Hugging Face's open-source transparency and IEEE's professional standards—point toward a future where AI agents are designed to enhance rather than undermine human autonomy and flourishing.

But that future isn't inevitable. The default trajectory, driven by competitive pressure and the path of least resistance, trends toward AI agents optimized for narrow metrics without sufficient attention to broader human values. Every day, organizations deploy AI systems without adequate consideration of how they might perpetuate bias, manipulate vulnerable users, erode privacy, or undermine human agency.

The alternative—human-centered AI design—requires sustained effort from multiple stakeholders:

- **Technologists and organizations** must move beyond treating ethics as compliance checkbox and instead embed human-centered principles throughout the design process. This means adopting frameworks like IEEE 7000, creating robust governance structures, ensuring diverse perspectives in development teams, and being willing to slow down or redesign systems when problems emerge.
- **Educators** must prepare the next generation of AI practitioners with both technical skills and ethical frameworks, not as separate domains but as integrated ways of thinking about technology's role in society.
- **Professional organizations** need to establish and enforce standards that make ethical AI development not just aspirational but expected, creating professional norms where failing to consider stakeholder values is seen as a mark of incompetence, not just a moral lapse.
- **Policymakers and regulators** must develop governance frameworks that incentivize human-centered design while avoiding crushing innovation, recognizing that effective regulation requires technical understanding and the flexibility to evolve as technology advances.
- **Citizens and communities** affected by AI agents must have mechanisms to voice concerns, contest decisions, and shape how systems operate in their lives and communities. Accountability requires that those affected by AI agents have power to hold developers and deployers responsible.

The technical challenge of building sophisticated AI agents has been met with great successes. Modern machine learning can create systems with remarkable capabilities. The hard problem now is ensuring those systems serve human values and enhance rather than diminish human agency. This isn't fundamentally a technical problem—it's a design problem, an organizational problem, and ultimately a moral problem.

The good news is that we already know much of what needs to be done. The frameworks exist. The examples of success demonstrate what's possible. The question is whether we'll muster the collective will to put that knowledge into practice before AI agents become so deeply woven into society's infrastructure that redesigning them becomes prohibitively difficult.

The next chapter examines what this means for individuals navigating a world increasingly shaped by AI agents, and how communities can organize to ensure these systems serve the public interest. But first, we must recognize that the future of AI agency isn't determined by the technology itself—it's determined by the choices we make about how to design and deploy it.

The engineers in Amazon's conference room thought they were building a meritocratic future. They learned, too late, that without intentional attention to human values, even sophisticated AI simply automates the inequities of the past. We can do better. We must do better. And, as the success stories in this chapter demonstrate, we know how.

CHAPTER 8

Reclaiming Human Agency

Elizabeth Richardson sat in her Chicago apartment on a cold January evening in 2023, staring at the rejection message on her phone. "We are currently not accepting housing choice vouchers." The words glowed blue against the screen's darkness, automated and absolute. She had found what seemed like the perfect place—a two-bedroom in a safe neighborhood with good schools for her kids, listed by Harbor Group Management. The rent was within her budget. The location was ideal. Everything was right except for one thing: she held a Section 8 housing voucher, and an AI chatbot had just rejected her application in seconds.

What Richardson didn't know was that her rejection wasn't the decision of a human landlord weighing her qualifications. Instead, a virtual assistant powered by PERQ AI had been programmed to automatically screen out anyone mentioning housing vouchers—before they could even schedule a viewing. Across the country, more than a hundred Harbor Group properties were using the same algorithmic gatekeeping, turning away thousands of applicants like Richardson without any human ever reviewing their credentials, their rental history, or their circumstances.[1]

But Richardson didn't accept the algorithmic verdict. She contacted Open Communities, an Evanston-based fair housing advocacy organization, and told them her story. What happened next would become a watershed moment in the fight to reclaim human agency from

C. Shah, *Agent Nation*, https://doi.org/10.1007/979-8-8688-2454-8_8

autonomous AI systems. Open Communities launched a six-month investigation, testing Harbor Group's chatbot across multiple properties and documenting how the AI systematically excluded voucher holders—a practice that, because Black families represent 85 percent of voucher recipients in the Chicago area, amounted to racial discrimination laundered through code.[2]

The case that followed exposed a crucial truth about the age of AI agents: these systems don't just assist human decision-making—they make decisions, enforce policies, and create barriers that can lock people out of opportunities entirely. And yet, when those decisions prove discriminatory or harmful, no human claims responsibility. The algorithm becomes a perfect shield, an autonomous actor operating in what accountability researchers call "the responsibility gap."

This is the paradox we face in Agent Nation. AI systems now make millions of consequential decisions daily—determining who gets housing, who gets hired, who receives medical care, and who passes their exams. These aren't hypothetical futures; they're present realities. But unlike the familiar debates about automation replacing jobs or algorithms invading privacy, this challenge runs deeper. It's about whether we, as individuals and communities, can maintain meaningful agency when artificial agents increasingly mediate our access to life's essentials.

The question isn't whether to use AI agents—that ship has sailed. The question is: How do we ensure these agents serve us rather than control us? How do we reclaim agency in a world where algorithms act as autonomous intermediaries between us and our goals?

The answer, as Richardson's case and countless others demonstrate, lies not in wholesale rejection of AI systems but in conscious, strategic engagement. It requires understanding how these agents operate, organizing collectively to challenge discriminatory algorithms, and building new frameworks for algorithmic accountability. This final chapter synthesizes the insights from our journey through Agent Nation into a practical roadmap for maintaining—and expanding—human agency in an age of artificial agents.

Understanding the Agent: Digital Literacy as Resistance

The first step in reclaiming agency is understanding how AI agents actually work. This isn't about becoming a data scientist or AI engineers; it's about developing what we might call algorithmic literacy—the ability to recognize when you're interacting with an AI system, understand its basic logic, and identify its weaknesses and biases.

Consider José Zamora, a job seeker in Los Angeles who spent months sending out 50 to 100 applications per day without receiving a single callback. His qualifications were solid, his experience was relevant. The problem, he suspected, wasn't what was on his resume—it was the name at the top. Zamora decided to run an experiment: he dropped one letter from his first name, changing "José" to "Joe." Everything else remained identical. Within a week, his inbox filled with interview requests.[3]

Zamora's experience, documented by BuzzFeed and reported across major media outlets, illustrated something that academic research had been demonstrating for years: the hiring process, whether mediated by humans or algorithms, is not neutral. A landmark study by economists Marianne Bertrand and Sendhil Mullainathan found that resumes with white-sounding names received 50 percent more callbacks than identical resumes with Black-sounding names—a gap equivalent to eight additional years of work experience.[4] The algorithmic gatekeepers that now screen applications for an estimated 99 percent of Fortune 500 companies have not eliminated this bias; in many cases, they have encoded it.

Research from the University of Washington, presented at the 2024 AAAI/ACM Conference on Artificial Intelligence, Ethics, and Society, examined how large language models used in hiring evaluate resumes. The findings were stark: across three state-of-the-art AI models and over 550 job descriptions, resumes with white-associated names were favored 85 percent of the time. The models never once ranked a resume with a Black male-associated name above one with a white male-associated name.[5] "The use of AI tools for hiring procedures is already widespread, and it's proliferating faster than we can regulate it," lead author Kyra Wilson observed. "Currently, outside of a New York City law, there's no regulatory, independent audit of these systems."[6]

This kind of algorithmic literacy—understanding that AI hiring systems may perpetuate rather than eliminate bias—is becoming essential across domains. Separate research from MIT has shown that AI writing assistance tools can help job seekers improve their applications, resulting in 7.8 percent more job offers and 8.4 percent higher wages.[7] But the core issue isn't whether candidates can game individual systems; it's that the systems themselves often encode discriminatory patterns that persist regardless of individual qualifications.

The research revealed something crucial: the AI hiring agents weren't necessarily identifying better candidates; they were identifying candidates who understood how to navigate algorithmic gatekeeping.[8]

This kind of algorithmic literacy is becoming essential across domains. In healthcare, patients who understand how AI diagnostic systems work—that they're pattern-matching tools trained on specific populations—can better advocate for second opinions when something doesn't feel right. In education, students who recognize the limitations of AI proctoring software—that it flags behavior based on statistical norms rather than actual cheating—can better challenge false accusations.

But individual literacy, while necessary, isn't sufficient. The burden of understanding opaque algorithmic systems shouldn't fall entirely on those subjected to them. This is where collective action becomes crucial.

Organizing Together: Collective Power Against Algorithmic Discrimination

Carmen Arroyo faced an impossible situation. Her son Mikhail had been severely injured in a 2015 accident while working atop a utility pole, falling 30 feet and sustaining injuries that left him unable to walk, speak, or care for himself. After months in rehabilitation, Carmen wanted to move him from a nursing home into her apartment in Windham, Connecticut, where she could serve as his primary caregiver. She applied to transfer to a two-bedroom unit in her same building. The landlord used CoreLogic's CrimSAFE screening software, which returned a single verdict: "disqualifying record."[9]

Neither Carmen nor the landlord knew what that record was. CoreLogic refused to provide details, demanding that Carmen produce a power of attorney signed by Mikhail—impossible given his disabilities. When attorneys from the Connecticut Fair Housing Center finally uncovered the truth, it was almost absurd: Mikhail had been arrested in Pennsylvania in 2014 for a minor retail theft charge that was ultimately dismissed. No conviction. No trial. Just an old arrest record that CoreLogic's algorithm had transformed into an insurmountable barrier to housing.[10]

What Carmen needed wasn't just persistence—it was power. In April 2018, the Connecticut Fair Housing Center and the National Housing Law Project filed a lawsuit that would become the first of its kind to directly challenge a tenant screening company for fair housing violations.[11] The legal theory was straightforward: because Black and Latino Americans are arrested, convicted, and incarcerated at disproportionately higher rates due to systemic inequities in the criminal justice system, using criminal records as automatic disqualifiers has a discriminatory "disparate impact" on these communities—even when no individual landlord or algorithm designer intends to discriminate.[12]

These weren't isolated incidents. They represented a broader pattern of algorithmic gatekeeping that fair housing organizations had documented across the country. The Government Accountability Office's July 2025 report on property technology in rental housing documented the rapid spread of algorithmic tools across the industry.[13] The report found that tenant screening, rent setting, advertising, and other rental housing activities are increasingly conducted through digital tools incorporating algorithms and artificial intelligence—raising significant concerns about potential discrimination. GAO noted that potential renters may struggle to understand, and property owners to explain, the basis for screening decisions made by algorithms. The report recommended enhanced federal oversight, particularly of facial recognition tools used in public housing, and documented ongoing enforcement actions against tenant screening companies for discriminatory practices and Fair Credit Reporting Act violations.[14]

But the collective response wasn't just legal action—it was also organizing for systemic change. In cities across America, tenant advocacy groups began building what they called "algorithmic accountability networks." These coalitions brought together affected individuals, fair housing organizations, legal aid societies, and technology researchers to document algorithmic discrimination, share strategies for challenging automated rejections and push for stronger regulation.

The power of collective organizing became particularly evident in the student movement against AI proctoring. When universities rushed to adopt online exam surveillance during the pandemic, students didn't just complain—they organized. At Western University in Ontario, students launched a campaign in 2020 that gathered more than 10,000 signatures demanding removal of Proctortrack after students documented the software's invasive surveillance practices and facial recognition failures.[15] While the university continued using Proctortrack through the 2020-21 academic year, sustained student pressure ultimately led Western to switch proctoring software providers in May 2021—a shift that demonstrated how organized resistance could force institutional change even when outright bans remained elusive.[16]

The movement gained momentum as students documented the harms. When law student Areeb Khan tried to sign into the online portal to take his practice bar exam, he was met with a strange message: "Due to poor lighting we are unable to identify your face." Additional lighting didn't solve the issue. Khan even tried signing in from the brightest room in his New York apartment—the bathroom. He began to suspect that it was his dark skin tone that rattled Examplify, the test proctoring platform.[17] His experience, reported by the *Christian Science Monitor,* illustrated a pattern that Black students had been describing for months: proctoring software calibrated for white skin was systematically failing to recognize their faces.

Student researchers turned these experiences into rigorous investigation. Akash Satheesan, a software researcher and college student whose university used Proctorio, analyzed the code behind the proctoring extension and found it was using facial detection models from OpenCV that failed to detect faces in images labeled as Black 57 percent of the time.[18] His findings, validated by VICE Motherboard and security researchers, demonstrated that the failures weren't random glitches—they were predictable consequences of facial recognition systems trained predominantly on lighter-skinned faces. As Shea Swauger, a university librarian researching proctoring software, documented in *MIT Technology Review:* "A Black woman at my university once told me that whenever she used Proctorio's test proctoring software, it always prompted her to shine more light on her face. The software couldn't validate her identity... Her white peers never had this problem."[19]

By 2024, the student movement had achieved tangible victories. More than 50 universities had either banned AI proctoring entirely or severely restricted its use. The protests also catalyzed broader conversations about surveillance in education and the ethics of using AI systems to monitor students in their homes—a practice that legal scholars argued violated reasonable expectations of privacy.[20]

These victories demonstrate a crucial principle: individuals facing algorithmic discrimination often lack the power to challenge systems on their own, but collective organizing can shift the balance. When people come together to document patterns of harm, share strategies, and demand accountability, they can force institutions and companies to change practices that would have persisted indefinitely if challenged only through individual complaints.

Demanding Transparency: Opening the Black Box

Understanding how to navigate algorithmic systems and organizing collectively to challenge discriminatory decisions both require one fundamental precondition: knowing how these systems actually work. Yet most AI agents operate as black boxes, their decision-making logic hidden behind claims of proprietary algorithms and trade secrets. Reclaiming agency therefore requires forcing open those boxes—demanding transparency as a prerequisite for accountability.

New York City's Local Law 144, passed in 2021 and with enforcement beginning July 5, 2023, provides a model for what algorithmic transparency can look like in practice.[21] The law, as explained in earlier chapters, requires employers using automated employment decision tools to conduct annual bias audits and publicly disclose the results. It mandates that job candidates must be informed when AI systems are being used to evaluate them and gives them the right to request information about how the algorithms work and what data they use.

The law's impact became evident as companies were forced to confront what their algorithms were actually doing. Bias audits revealed patterns of disparate impact that had been invisible when systems operated as black boxes. Research from the University of Washington demonstrated the scale of the problem: AI hiring models consistently favored white-associated names over Black-associated names and male names over female names across multiple occupations and AI systems.[22]

Crucially, the transparency requirement didn't just reveal problems—it created pressure to fix them. Companies that wanted to continue using AI hiring tools had to redesign their systems to pass bias audits. By 2024, several major AI vendors had fundamentally restructured their products, incorporating fairness constraints and demographic parity checks. The transparency mandate transformed the market, making non-discriminatory design a competitive necessity rather than an optional enhancement.

Similar dynamics emerged in other domains. California's AI transparency requirements for healthcare systems, implemented in 2023, forced medical AI vendors to disclose the demographic composition of their training data. The revelations were sobering: diagnostic algorithms used in hospitals across the state had been trained predominantly on data from white patients, with some systems having less than 5 percent representation from Black, Latino, and Asian populations. Armed with this information, patient advocacy groups successfully pressured hospitals to either improve the diversity of training data or add explicit warnings about the AI's limitations for certain patient populations.

The pushback against transparency often invokes trade secrets and competitive advantage. But transparency doesn't require revealing source code or proprietary algorithms. What it requires is meaningful information: What factors does the system consider? What data was it trained on? How accurate is it for different demographic groups? How can its decisions be appealed? These are questions that can be answered without compromising legitimate business interests—and that must be answered if AI agents are to be held accountable.

Building Democratic Oversight: From Corporate Control to Public Governance

Even with transparency, individual and collective action can only go so far. When AI agents make consequential decisions affecting millions of people—determining creditworthiness, allocating public benefits, setting insurance premiums, screening job applicants—those decisions take on a quasi-governmental character. They shape access to opportunity and distribute life chances. Such power demands democratic oversight.

The concept isn't radical; it's recognizing that AI agents increasingly perform functions that would be subject to democratic accountability if performed by government agencies. When algorithms decide who qualifies for housing assistance, they're exercising power analogous to welfare administrators—power that in a democratic society should be subject to public deliberation, legislative oversight, and judicial review.

This principle found expression in the European Union's AI Act, which took effect in 2024 and established the world's most comprehensive framework for democratic AI governance. The Act categorizes AI systems by risk level and subjects high-risk systems—those affecting employment, education, law enforcement, and access to essential services—to stringent requirements, including human oversight, transparency obligations, and regulatory approval before deployment.

But democratic governance doesn't have to come from top-down regulation alone. Civil society organizations have proven that community pressure can force accountability even from national governments. In the Netherlands, a broad coalition of human rights and welfare rights groups, joined by concerned citizens, sued the Dutch government in 2018 over its System Risk Indication (SyRI)—an algorithm that cross-referenced personal data to identify citizens supposedly more likely to commit welfare fraud. SyRI had been deployed exclusively in low-income neighborhoods with predominantly minority residents, operating as what the UN Special Rapporteur on extreme poverty called an attempt to "spy on the poor."[23]

In February 2020, the Hague District Court issued a landmark ruling: SyRI violated the European Convention on Human Rights.[24] The court found that the system lacked sufficient safeguards against privacy invasion, including a "serious lack of transparency about its functioning." Without more information about how SyRI worked, the court warned, the system "may discriminate on the basis of socio-economic or migrant status." The ruling was the first time a court anywhere had stopped the use of digital technologies by welfare authorities on human rights grounds.[25]

The SyRI case demonstrated a crucial principle: algorithmic systems affecting vulnerable populations can be successfully challenged through coordinated legal and advocacy efforts. It also revealed the scale of harm that goes undetected when such systems operate without oversight. Just months after the SyRI ruling, the Dutch childcare benefits scandal erupted, revealing that a related algorithmic system had falsely accused nearly 35,000 parents—most of whom were migrants or children of migrants—of defrauding the benefits system. Families were pushed into debt and poverty. The scandal ultimately led the entire Dutch government to resign in January 2021.[26]

These models of democratic governance represent a fundamental shift from treating AI as a purely technical domain to recognizing it as a political one—as a set of systems that embody values, distribute power, and shape social outcomes. When such systems are left entirely to corporate discretion or expert technocrats, they inevitably reflect the perspectives and interests of those who build them. Democratic oversight provides a mechanism for broader social values and community needs to influence algorithmic design.

Maintaining the Human in the Loop: AI as Tool, Not Replacement

Perhaps the most fundamental strategy for reclaiming agency is insisting that AI agents remain tools that augment human judgment rather than autonomous systems that replace it. This isn't just about preserving jobs—it's about recognizing that certain decisions require human qualities that no algorithm possesses: contextual understanding, empathy, ethical reasoning, and accountability.

In healthcare, this principle has gained traction through movements for AI-assisted rather than AI-driven decision-making. Research on AI-assisted medical decision-making has consistently found that the most effective implementations treat AI as a consultative tool rather than a replacement for physician judgment. A comprehensive 2024 review published in *BMC Medical Informatics and Decision Making* emphasized that successful AI integration maintains clear role distinctions: AI systems excel at pattern recognition and processing large datasets, while humans provide contextual understanding, ethical judgment, and accountability.[27] When these complementary capabilities are properly integrated, with humans maintaining ultimate decision-making authority, outcomes improve for both efficiency and patient wellbeing.

Counteracting automation bias requires deliberate system design. Researchers have recommended that AI diagnostic tools should present their reasoning and confidence levels, highlight cases where the algorithm's training data was limited, and prompt physicians to identify factors the AI might have missed.[28] The healthcare field has made progress in developing frameworks for AI-assisted shared decision-making that explicitly preserves patient agency. Research published in the *Journal of Medical Internet Research* found that when AI diagnostic tools were designed to facilitate conversation between doctors and patients rather than provide definitive answers, patient satisfaction increased significantly and patients reported feeling more involved in their care decisions.[29] The key difference was treating the AI as one source of information in a collaborative process rather than as an authoritative oracle.[30]

This model of human-AI collaboration provides a template for other domains. In hiring, AI can screen applications for basic qualifications, but humans should make final decisions considering factors algorithms can't assess—motivation, cultural fit, potential for growth. In criminal justice, risk assessment tools can identify statistical patterns, but judges should retain discretion to consider individual circumstances that no algorithm captures. In education, AI can flag patterns of struggle, but teachers should determine appropriate interventions based on knowledge of individual students.

The principle is simple but powerful: AI agents should augment human agency, not replace it. When we treat algorithms as decision-makers rather than decision-support tools, we don't just risk bad outcomes—we abdicate the very human responsibility that gives decisions moral weight and makes accountability possible.

The Path Forward: From Resistance to Reconstruction

These strategies—developing algorithmic literacy, organizing collectively, demanding transparency, building democratic oversight, and maintaining human judgment—aren't separate responses but interconnected elements of a comprehensive approach to reclaiming agency in Agent Nation. Each reinforces the others: transparency enables collective organizing, which creates political pressure for democratic oversight, which in turn establishes the conditions for meaningful human judgment.

Together, they point toward a fundamental reframing of our relationship with AI agents. The dominant narrative treats algorithmic systems as inevitable forces—as though their deployment and design are natural processes beyond human control. But as every case in this chapter demonstrates, nothing about these systems is inevitable. They embody choices: choices about what to optimize, whose interests to serve, and how to distribute power and opportunity.

Richardson's housing discrimination case resulted in a landmark settlement in 2024. Harbor Group Management agreed not only to pay damages but to completely redesign its tenant screening processes, adding human review for all voucher holders and conducting regular audits for bias. More significantly, the settlement required Harbor Group to support fair housing advocacy by funding community education about algorithmic discrimination—turning the company that perpetuated harm into a resource for preventing future harm.[31]

The case's ripple effects extended far beyond Harbor Group. Following the settlement, several major property management companies voluntarily revised their AI screening policies. Industry groups developed new standards for algorithmic fairness in tenant screening. And housing advocates in cities across the country used Richardson's victory as a template for challenging discriminatory algorithms, filing dozens of similar complaints and lawsuits.[32]

But perhaps the most significant outcome was cultural: Richardson's case helped shift the conversation from treating algorithmic discrimination as an unfortunate side effect of innovation to recognizing it as a civil rights violation that demands the same response as any other form of illegal discrimination. It demonstrated that the fact that discrimination happens through code rather than conscious human bias doesn't make it less harmful or less actionable.

This is the central lesson of Agent Nation: AI agents are powerful, but they're not beyond challenge or control. They operate with authority we grant them, whether actively or through acquiescence. And that authority can be reclaimed—not through wholesale rejection of algorithmic systems, but through deliberate choices about how we design, deploy, and govern them.

The future we're building isn't predetermined. It's a product of choices being made right now in corporate boardrooms, legislative chambers, courtrooms, and communities. Every time someone questions an algorithmic decision rather than accepting it as final, every time a community organizes to challenge discriminatory systems, every time regulators establish oversight mechanisms or companies choose to prioritize fairness over efficiency, we shape what Agent Nation becomes.

The stakes couldn't be higher. We're at an inflection point where the systems we build and the norms we establish today will structure power relationships for decades to come. The question is whether those systems will serve democratic values and human flourishing, or whether they'll encode and amplify existing inequalities while insulating them from challenge behind the veil of algorithmic objectivity.

What makes this moment both challenging and hopeful is that the answers aren't yet locked in. Unlike previous technological revolutions that unfolded over centuries, allowing institutions and norms to gradually adapt, the AI transformation is happening at unprecedented speed. But that same speed means we still have time to shape trajectories that aren't yet solidified into permanent infrastructure.

The pathway forward requires recognizing that questions about AI agents aren't primarily technical questions—they're political, ethical, and social questions about how we want to organize society, distribute power, and relate to one another. The technical capabilities exist to build AI systems that enhance rather than undermine human agency. What's required is the collective will to demand such systems and the institutional frameworks to make that demand effective.

This book has explored Agent Nation across eight dimensions—how AI agents operate in employment, education, healthcare, criminal justice, finance, consumer markets, democratic governance, and now, in the daily project of maintaining human agency itself. Across all these domains, a consistent pattern emerges: AI agents acquire power not through their own capacity but through the authority we grant them and the systems we build around them.

That power can be reclaimed, but only through deliberate action. Individual strategies like algorithmic literacy help people navigate systems as they exist. Collective organizing creates the power to challenge and change discriminatory algorithms. Transparency requirements open black boxes, making bias visible and actionable. Democratic oversight mechanisms ensure that consequential AI systems serve public values rather than purely private interests. And maintaining meaningful human judgment in high-stakes decisions preserves accountability and ethical reasoning that no algorithm can replicate.

These aren't abstract principles or distant aspirations. They're concrete strategies being implemented right now in cities, courtrooms, legislatures, and communities across the world. Each represents a choice to treat AI agents as tools subject to human governance rather than as autonomous forces beyond human control.

The examples throughout this book—and particularly in this final chapter—aren't meant to provide a comprehensive solution to the challenges of Agent Nation. They're meant to demonstrate that solutions are possible, that resistance is effective, and that the future of AI in society remains open to contestation and reconstruction.

What they require from all of us—as workers, consumers, patients, students, citizens—is a fundamental shift in how we relate to algorithmic systems. We must move from passive acceptance to active engagement, from individual adaptation to collective organizing, from treating algorithms as inevitable to recognizing them as constructed and contestable.

Agent Nation isn't a future we're approaching—it's a present reality we're already inhabiting. The question we face isn't whether AI agents will be part of society's infrastructure but what kind of agents they'll be, whose interests they'll serve, and how much power they'll wield relative to human communities. These aren't questions with technical answers. They're questions that demand democratic deliberation, collective action, and sustained vigilance.

The path forward won't be easy. Powerful interests benefit from the current system where algorithmic decisions can't be effectively challenged, where black boxes shield discriminatory practices from accountability, and where efficiency trumps fairness. Reclaiming agency will require persistent effort, creative strategies, and willingness to challenge systems that present themselves as inevitable or optimal.

But the examples in this chapter—Richardson securing housing and Arroyo defeating discriminatory screening—show that such challenges can succeed. They demonstrate that individuals and communities have more power than they often realize to question algorithmic authority, expose discriminatory systems, and force accountability.

Most fundamentally, they prove that AI agents operate most powerfully when we treat their decisions as inevitable, when we accept algorithmic judgments as final, when we believe that technical systems are beyond challenge or change. The moment we question those assumptions—the moment we recognize that algorithms embody choices and that choices can be contested—agent power begins to shift back toward human communities.

This is ultimately what reclaiming human agency means: refusing to accept that algorithmic systems are neutral arbiters or inevitable forces, and instead recognizing them as human constructions that can be examined, challenged, redesigned, and governed according to human values. It means treating transparency not as a nice-to-have feature but as a prerequisite for accountability. It means organizing collectively because individual complaints rarely change systems. It means demanding democratic oversight over consequential AI systems because such oversight is how democratic societies govern power.

And it means maintaining human judgment in contexts that require empathy, ethical reasoning, contextual understanding, and accountability—qualities no algorithm possesses and no amount of training data can replicate.

The choices we make in the next few years about AI governance, algorithmic accountability, and the balance between artificial and human agency will shape society for decades. We can build systems that enhance human capability while preserving human control, that improve efficiency without sacrificing fairness, that harness AI's power while maintaining democratic governance. But such systems won't emerge automatically from technological progress—they'll emerge from deliberate choices to prioritize human agency over algorithmic convenience.

Agent Nation is here. The question isn't whether to live with AI agents but how to live with them—whether as subjects of algorithmic systems beyond our control, or as citizens who maintain sovereignty over the technological systems that mediate our lives. That choice remains fundamentally in human hands, even now. The power to shape our algorithmic future hasn't been ceded to machines. It's been granted to them, which means it can also be reclaimed.

Elizabeth Richardson reclaimed her power by refusing to accept an algorithmic verdict as final. By taking that first step—questioning rather than accepting—she set in motion a cascade of changes that benefited not just herself but thousands of other housing seekers facing similar algorithmic gatekeeping. Her story illustrates the central message of this book: in Agent Nation, human agency persists not as a passive condition but as an active practice, sustained through countless individual choices to question, organize, demand accountability, and insist that machines remain tools serving human values rather than autonomous actors beyond human governance.

The algorithmic future is being written right now, in courtrooms and city councils, in corporate boardrooms and community organizing meetings, in legislative chambers and classroom protests. What that future looks like depends on whether we accept algorithmic authority as inevitable or recognize it as constructed—and therefore contestable. The power to shape Agent Nation remains, fundamentally and irreducibly, a human power. The question is whether we'll exercise it.

References

Chapter 1

1. SEC Report, "Knight Capital Group, LLC," August 1, 2012. Securities and Exchange Commission Administrative Proceeding File No. 3-15570, October 16, 2013.

2. Dolfing, Henrico. "Case Study: The $440 Million Software Error at Knight Capital," Project Management Case Studies, 2019.

3. Nanex Market Data Analysis, "Knight Capital Group Trading Volume Analysis," August 1, 2012.

4. SEC Administrative Order, "In the Matter of Knight Capital Group, LLC," File No. 3-15570, October 16, 2013.

5. Joyce, Thomas. Interview with Bloomberg Television, August 2, 2012.

6. Lee, Won-Suk, et al. "Assessing Concordance With Watson for Oncology, a Cognitive Computing Decision Support System for Colon Cancer Treatment in Korea." *JCO Clinical Cancer Informatics,* Vol. 2, 2018, pp. 1-8.

7. Ross, Casey and Ike Swetlitz. "IBM's Watson recommended 'unsafe and incorrect' cancer treatments, internal documents show," STAT News, July 25, 2018.

C. Shah, *Agent Nation,* https://doi.org/10.1007/979-8-8688-2454-8

8. Strickland, Eliza. "IBM Watson, heal thyself: How IBM overpromised and underdelivered on AI health care," *IEEE Spectrum,* April 2019.

9. Ali, Muhammad, Piotr Sapiezynski, Miranda Bogen, Aleksandra Korolova, Alan Mislove, Aaron Rieke. 2019. "Discrimination through Optimization: How Facebook's Ad Delivery Can Lead to Biased Outcomes," Proceedings of the ACM on Human-Computer Interaction 3 (CSCW): 1-30. https://doi.org/10.1145/3359301.

10. Upturn and Leadership Conference on Civil and Human Rights. 2014 "Civil Rights, Big Data, and Our Algorithmic Future," September 2014, pp. 23-26.

11. U.S. Department of Justice, "Justice Department Secures Groundbreaking Settlement Agreement with Meta Platforms, Inc.," Press Release, June 21, 2022. www.justice.gov/usao-sdny/pr/united-states-attorney-resolves-groundbreaking-suit-against-meta-platforms-inc-formerly

12. American Civil Liberties Union, "ACLU and Workers Take On Facebook for Gender Discrimination in Job Ads," ACLU Press Release, September 18, 2018, www.aclu.org/press-releases/aclu-and-workers-take-facebook-gender-discrimination-job-ads

13. Smart Nation Singapore. "A Thriving Digital Future for All." Smart Nation Singapore Official Website, 2024. www.smartnation.gov.sg/

14. CNBC. "Singapore invests heavily in tech and innovation as it seeks to become a 'smart nation.'" CNBC Video, September 25, 2020. www.cnbc.com/video/2020/09/25/singapore-invests-in-tech-as-it-seeks-to-become-a-smart-nation.html

15. Bay, Jason, "Automated contact tracing is not a coronavirus panacea," *Medium*, April 11, 2020.

16. Singapore Government. "Hawker Centres Transformation Programme (HTP)," SG101.gov.sg, 2021. www.sg101.gov.sg/resources/connexionsg/evenbettersingaporeshawkercentres/

17. Kirilenko, Andrei, et al. "The Flash Crash: High-Frequency Trading in an Electronic Market," *Journal of Finance*, Vol. 72, No. 3, 2017.

18. Russell, Stuart, and Peter Norvig. *Artificial Intelligence: A Modern Approach*, 4th Edition, Pearson, 2020.

19. CFTC Report, "Findings Regarding the Market Events of May 6, 2010," September 30, 2010

20. McKinsey & Company. "Beyond automation: How gen AI is reshaping supply chains," McKinsey Talks Operations, April 17, 2025. www.mckinsey.com/capabilities/operations/our-insights/beyond-automation-how-gen-ai-is-reshaping-supply-chains

21. Zuboff, Shoshana. *The Age of Surveillance Capitalism*, PublicAffairs, 2019.

22. United for Smart Sustainable Cities (U4SSC) / International Telecommunication Union. "Guiding Principles for Artificial Intelligence in Cities." ITU U4SSC Deliverable, 2024. `https://u4ssc.itu.int/guiding-principles/`

23. Kalra, Nidhi and David G. Groves. "The Enemy of Good: Estimating the Cost of Waiting for Nearly Perfect Automated Vehicles." RAND Corporation, RR-2150-RC, November 2017. `www.rand.org/pubs/research_reports/RR2150.html`

24. CFTC-SEC Joint Report, "Findings Regarding the Market Events of May 6, 2010," September 30, 2010.

25. Strickland, Eliza. "IBM Watson, heal thyself: How IBM overpromised and underdelivered on AI health care," *IEEE Spectrum,* April 2, 2019.

26. O'Neil, Cathy. *Weapons of Math Destruction: How Big Data Increases Inequality and Threatens Democracy,* Crown Publishers, 2016.

Chapter 2

1. Kammerer, Rachel. "The Legal Implications of Artificial Intelligence Video Interviews," *Iowa Law Review,* Vol. 107, 2023.

2. HR Dive, "AI hiring software was biased against deaf employees, ACLU alleges in ADA case," March 24, 2025.

3. Ibid.

4. Public Justice, "Complaint Filed Against Intuit and HireVue Over Biased AI Hiring Technology That Violates Colorado Anti-Discrimination Act, ADA, and Title VII," March 19, 2025. www.publicjustice.net/hirevue-intuit-artificial-intelligence-biased-hiring/

5. MIT Technology Review, "The AI hiring industry is under scrutiny—but it'll be hard to fix," November 7, 2019. www.technologyreview.com/2019/11/07/75194/hirevue-ai-automated-hiring-discrimination-ftc-epic-bias/

6. *Washington Post,* "Rights group files federal complaint against AI-hiring firm HireVue, citing 'unfair and deceptive' practices," November 6, 2019.

7. *Cardozo Law Review,* "Automating Discrimination: AI Hiring Practices and Gender Inequality," 2024.

8. *Washington Post,* "Rights group files federal complaint against AI-hiring firm HireVue, citing 'unfair and deceptive' practices," November 6, 2019.

9. EPIC, "In re HireVue," FTC Complaint filed November 6, 2019.

10. MIT Technology Review, "The AI hiring industry is under scrutiny—but it'll be hard to fix," November 7, 2019. www.technologyreview.com/2019/11/07/75194/hirevue-ai-automated-hiring-discrimination-ftc-epic-bias/

11. UC Berkeley School of Information, "Amazon's ADAPT and its Harm on Workers," March 2, 2022.

12. CBS News, "Amazon under fire for software that recommends firing workers," April 26, 2019; *MIT Technology Review,* "Amazon's system for tracking its warehouse workers can automatically fire them," May 19, 2022.

13. Kantor, Jodi et al. "Inside Amazon's Employment Machine." *The New York Times,* June 15, 2021.

14. *MIT Technology Review,* "Amazon's system for tracking its warehouse workers can automatically fire them," May 19, 2022.

15. UC Berkeley School of Information, "Amazon's ADAPT and its Harm on Workers," March 2, 2022.

16. The American Prospect, "Amazon Uses Arsenal of AI Weapons Against Workers," March 12, 2025.

17. Ibid.

18. The Register, "Amazon accused of using algorithms to push warehouse workers to breaking point," March 18, 2025. `www.theregister.com/2025/03/18/amazon_algorithmic_worker_management/`

19. The American Prospect, "Amazon Uses Arsenal of AI Weapons Against Workers," March 12, 2025.

20. Ibid.

21. HRD Connect, "Amazon's latest faux par questions the ethics of employee surveillance," August 5, 2024.

22. CNIL (Commission Nationale de l'Informatique et des Libertés), "Employee monitoring: CNIL fined AMAZON FRANCE LOGISTIQUE €32 million," January 23, 2024; CNBC, "French regulator fines Amazon unit $35 million for 'excessively intrusive' employee surveillance," January 30, 2024.
23. Slate, "Uber and Lyft: Why A.I.-powered wages of gig workers may be coming for your office job," October 13, 2024.
24. CBC News, "Uber started using 'algorithmic pricing' in Canada. Is that a good or bad thing?" October 14, 2024.
25. Slate, "Uber and Lyft: Why A.I.-powered wages of gig workers may be coming for your office job," October 13, 2024.
26. Dubal, Veena. "Algorithmic Wage Discrimination," Columbia Law Review, Vol. 123, 2023
27. *San Francisco Chronicle,* "AI is making it harder for Uber and Lyft drivers to earn a living," January 2025.
28. CBC News, "Uber started using 'algorithmic pricing' in Canada. Is that a good or bad thing?" October 14, 2024.
29. National Employment Law Project, "Uber's Price-Gouging and What We Can Do About It," November 14, 2024.
30. *San Francisco Chronicle,* "AI is making it harder for Uber and Lyft drivers to earn a living," January 2025.
31. Ibid.

32. Slate, "Uber and Lyft: Why A.I.-powered wages of gig workers may be coming for your office job," October 13, 2024.

33. Wells, Katie and Ustek-Spilda, Funda. "Uber for Nursing: How an AI-Powered Gig Model Is Threatening Health Care," Roosevelt Institute, June 23, 2025.

34. LPE Project, "Nursing on Demand: The Gig Economy Comes for Health Care," June 30, 2025.

35. Doctorow, Cory. "Nurses whose shitty boss is a shitty app," Pluralistic, December 18, 2024.

36. Common Dreams, "New Report Sheds Light on the Pitfalls of AI-Powered 'Gig Nursing,'" December 19, 2024.

37. STAT News, "The gig economy has come for nursing," March 31, 2025.

38. Thomson Reuters Foundation, "Uber for nurses? US health workers turn to gig work," December 13, 2023.

39. *TIME*, "How to Get a Six-Figure Job as an AI Prompt Engineer," April 14, 2023.

40. Ibid.

41. Ibid.

42. Ibid.

43. PromptLayer Blog, "AI Prompt Engineering Jobs in 2025: Skills, Salaries & Future Outlook," August 21, 2025.

44. ZipRecruiter, "AI Prompt Engineer Jobs," September 2025.

45. Bank of America. "BofA's Erica Surpasses 2 Billion Interactions, Helping 42 Million Clients Since Launch." Press release, April 8, 2024. https://newsroom.bankofamerica.com/content/newsroom/press-releases/2024/04/bofa-s-erica-surpasses-2-billion-interactions--helping-42-millio.html

46. Klarna. "Klarna AI Assistant Handles Two-Thirds of Customer Service Chats in Its First Month." Press release, February 27, 2024. Cited in Kathryn Moody, "Replaced by AI? Klarna News May Confirm Workers' Worst Fears," HR Dive, February 29, 2024. https://www.hrdive.com/news/klarna-ai-replacing-workers/708971/

47. Sherin Shibu, "Klarna Is Hiring Customer Service Agents After AI Couldn't Cut It on Calls, According to the Company's CEO," Entrepreneur, May 9, 2025. www.entrepreneur.com/business-news/klarna-ceo-reverses-course-by-hiring-more-humans-not-ai/491396

48. SightCall. "Reduce Contact Center Turnover By Managing Emotional Labor." March 6, 2025. https://sightcall.com/blog/reduce-contact-center-turnover-by-managing-emotional-labor/

49. U.S. Bureau of Labor Statistics. "Customer Service Representatives: Occupational Outlook Handbook." Updated August 29, 2024. www.bls.gov/ooh/office-and-administrative-support/customer-service-representatives.htm

50. Privacy International, "Humans in the AI loop: the data labelers behind some of the most powerful LLMs' training datasets," 2024.

51. *Rolling Stone,* "Bestiality and Beyond: ChatGPT Works Because Underpaid Workers Read About Horrible Things," January 18, 2023.

52. Ibid.

53. Ibid.

54. Ibid.

55. "The Gruelling, Low-Paid Human Work behind Generative AI Curtain." Agence France-Presse, October 17, 2025. `www.canadianaffairs.news/2025/10/17/the-gruelling-low-paid-human-work-behind-generative-ai-curtain/`

56. Lesley Stahl. "Kenyan Workers with AI Jobs Thought They Had Tickets to the Future until the Grim Reality Set In." CBS News / 60 Minutes, November 25, 2024. `www.cbsnews.com/news/ai-work-kenya-exploitation-60-minutes/`

57. Privacy International. "Humans in the AI Loop: The Data Labelers behind Some of the Most Powerful LLMs' Training Datasets." 2024. `https://privacyinternational.org/explainer/5357/humans-ai-loop-data-labelers-behind-some-most-powerful-llms-training-datasets`

58. Qhala, "Data Workers in AI: A New Frontier of Labour Exploitation in the Global South," *Medium,* June 10, 2025.

59. Privacy International, "Humans in the AI loop: the data labelers behind some of the most powerful LLMs' training datasets," 2024.

60. *NOEMA Magazine,* "The Exploited Labor Behind Artificial Intelligence," October 13, 2022.

61. Ibid.

62. *Computer Weekly,* "Kenyan AI workers form Data Labelers Association," 2025

63. Final Call News, "Exploitation and rising concerns facing Kenyan AI data labeling workers," December 2, 2024.

64. Winsome Marketing, "Google's Mass Firing of Over 200 AI Contractors," January 2025

65. Ibid.

66. *Computer Weekly,* "Kenyan AI workers form Data Labelers Association," 2025.

67. Winsome Marketing, "Google's Mass Firing of Over 200 AI Contractors," January 2025.

68. The American Prospect, "Amazon Uses Arsenal of AI Weapons Against Workers," March 12, 2025.

69. National Nurses United, "Nurses and Patients' Bill of Rights: Guiding Principles for A.I. Justice in Nursing and Health Care," May 2024, `www.nationalnursesunited.org/sites/default/files/nnu/documents/0424_NursesPatients-BillOfRights_Principles-AI-Justice_flyer.pdf`.

70. New York State Nurses Association, "A 'Virtual' Attack on Our Union Voice," accessed January 2026, www.nysna.org/new-york-nurse/virtual-attack-our-union-voice

71. National Nurses United, "Risky Business," *National Nurse* magazine, June 10, 2024, www.nationalnursesunited.org/article/risky-business.

72. Baker McKenzie, "Navigating Labor's Response to AI," June 2025, www.bakermckenzie.com/en/insight/publications/2025/06/navigating-labors-response-to-ai.

73. Billy Perrigo, "150 African Workers for AI Companies Vote to Unionize," *TIME*, May 1, 2023, https://time.com/6275995/chatgpt-facebook-african-workers-union/.

74. Nita Bhalla, "Mental Trauma: African Content Moderators Push Big Tech on Rights," Thomson Reuters Foundation / Context, October 16, 2023, www.context.news/big-tech/mental-trauma-african-content-moderators-push-big-tech-on-rights.

75. Marina Rafaela, "In Nairobi's Silicon Savanna, African Workers Are Taking on Big Tech," *Coda Story*, August 6, 2025, www.codastory.com/authoritarian-tech/kenya-content-moderators/.

Chapter 3

1. Loomis v. Wisconsin, 881 N.W.2d 749 (Wis. 2016).
2. ProPublica, "Machine Bias: There's Software Used Across the Country to Predict Future Criminals. And It's Biased Against Blacks," May 23, 2016.
3. Loomis v. Wisconsin, 881 N.W.2d 749 (Wis. 2016).
4. Ibid.
5. Ibid.
6. Electronic Privacy Information Center, "EPIC v. DOJ (Criminal Justice Algorithms)," https://epic.org/documents/epic-v-doj-criminal-justice-algorithms/
7. City of Chicago, Office of Inspector General, "Review of the Chicago Police Department's 'Predictive Risk Models,'" January 23, 2020, https://igchicago.org/2020/01/23/review-of-the-chicago-police-departments-predictive-risk-models/; Jeremy Gorner and Annie Sweeney, "For Years Chicago Police Rated the Risk of Tens of Thousands Being Caught Up in Violence. That Controversial Effort Has Quietly Been Ended," *Chicago Tribune*, January 25, 2020, www.chicagotribune.com/news/criminal-justice/ct-chicago-police-strategic-subject-list-ended-20200125-spn4kjmrxrh4tmktdjckhtox4i-story.html.

8. City of Chicago Data Portal, "Strategic Subject List - Historical," accessed January 2026, https://data.cityofchicago.org/Public-Safety/Strategic-Subject-List-Historical/4aki-r3np. The official documentation states: "Based on this time frame's version of the Strategic Subject Algorithm, individuals with criminal records are ranked using eight attributes, not including race or sex."

9. Brianna Posadas, "How Strategic Is Chicago's 'Strategic Subjects List'? Upturn Investigates," *Medium* (Equal Future), June 26, 2017, https://medium.com/equal-future/how-strategic-is-chicagos-strategic-subjects-list-upturn-investigates-9e5b4b235a7c; "Chicago Police Department Ends Use of 'Strategic Subject List,'" *Chicago Sun-Times*, January 27, 2020, https://chicago.suntimes.com/city-hall/2020/1/27/21084030/chicago-police-strategic-subject-list-party-to-violence-inspector-general-joe-ferguson.

10. Yana Kunichoff and Patrick Sier, "The Contradictions of Chicago Police's Secretive List," *Chicago Magazine*, August 21, 2017, https://www.chicagomag.com/city-life/august-2017/chicago-police-strategic-subject-list/. The investigation found that while geographic information was not directly included in the SSL, "the data shows that the most recent arrests of people with an SSL score map directly on the areas that are heavily policed."

11. Jeremy Gorner, "Chicago Police Use 'Heat List' as Strategy to Prevent Violence," *Chicago Tribune*, August 21, 2013, www.chicagotribune.com/2013/08/21/chicago-police-use-heat-list-as-strategy-to-prevent-violence/; University of Chicago Legal Forum, "Constraining Big Brother: The Legal Deficiencies Surrounding Chicago's Use of the Strategic Subject List," 2018, https://legal-forum.uchicago.edu/print-archive/constraining-big-brother-legal-deficiencies-surrounding-chicagos-use-strategic.

12. Ibid

13. Matt Stroud, "Heat Listed," *The Verge*, May 24, 2021, www.theverge.com/c/22444020/chicago-pd-predictive-policing-heat-list. Stroud's investigation documented that McDaniel believes "the heat list caused the harm its creators hoped to avoid: it predicted a shooting that wouldn't have happened if it hadn't predicted the shooting."

14. Jessica Saunders, Priscillia Hunt, and John S. Hollywood, "Predictions Put into Practice: A Quasi-Experimental Evaluation of Chicago's Predictive Policing Pilot," *Journal of Experimental Criminology* 12 (2016): 347–371; "Predictive Policing and the Long Road to Transparency," *South Side Weekly*, February 16, 2018, https://southsideweekly.com/predictive-policing-long-road-transparency/.

15. Kunichoff and Sier, “Contradictions of Chicago Police’s Secretive List.” The article notes that “there’s very little information available about how police are using the list” and describes how journalists obtained the data only after legal action.

16. Kunichoff and Sier, “Contradictions of Chicago Police’s Secretive List”; Michelle Mahon, National Nurses United, quoted in “National Nurses United Pushes Back Against Deployment of ‘Unproven’ AI in Healthcare,” *Fierce Healthcare,* June 4, 2024.

17. City of Chicago, Office of Inspector General, “Review of the Chicago Police Department’s ‘Predictive Risk Models’”; Gorner and Sweeney, “For Years Chicago Police Rated the Risk.” The OIG report identified concerns including “interventions influenced by PTV risk models which may have attached negative consequences to arrests that did not result in convictions.”

18. Andrew Guthrie Ferguson, *The Rise of Big Data Policing: Surveillance, Race, and the Future of Law Enforcement* (New York: NYU Press, 2017); “The Lessons of Chicago’s Disastrous ‘Crime Prediction’ Experiment,” *Filter,* March 12, 2020, `https://filtermag.org/chicago-crime-prediction/`.

19. New York City, “Automated Decision Systems Task Force,” NYC.gov, accessed January 2026, `www.nyc.gov/site/adstaskforce/index.page`; Rashida Richardson, ed., “Confronting Black Boxes: A Shadow Report of the New York City Automated Decision System Task Force” (New York:

AI Now Institute, December 4, 2019), https://ainowinstitute.org/publication/confronting-black-boxes-a-shadow-report-of-the-new-york-city-automated.

20. Nikki Davidson, "NYC's Data-Driven Future: 46 Algorithms and Counting," Government Technology, August 1, 2024, www.govtech.com/biz/data/nycs-data-driven-future-46-algorithms-and-counting.

21. Mary Louis, et al. v. SafeRent Solutions, et al., Case No. 1:22-CV-10800 (D. Mass. filed Aug. 26, 2022).

22. National Consumer Law Center, "SafeRent Solutions Accused of Illegally Discriminating Against Black and Hispanic Rental Applicants," press release, May 25, 2022, www.nclc.org/saferent-solution-accused-of-illegally-discriminating-against-black-and-hispanic-rental-applicants/.

23. Ibid.; American Bar Association, "Ghosts in the Machine: How Past and Present Biases Haunt Algorithmic Tenant Screening Systems," Human Rights, June 2024, www.americanbar.org/groups/crsj/resources/human-rights/2024-june/how-past-present-biases-haunt-algorithmic-tenant-screening-systems/.

24. U.S. Department of Justice, "Justice Department Files Statement of Interest in Fair Housing Act Case Alleging Unlawful Algorithm-Based Tenant Screening Practices," press release, January 9, 2023, www.justice.gov/archives/opa/pr/justice-department-files-statement-interest-fair-housing-act-case-alleging-unlawful-algorithm.

25. Associated Press, "Class Action Lawsuit on AI-Related Discrimination Reaches Final Settlement," Claims Journal, November 22, 2024, www.claimsjournal.com/news/national/2024/11/22/327550.htm.

26. Colin Lecher, "The NYC Algorithm Deciding Which Families Are Under Watch for Child Abuse," The Markup, May 20, 2025, https://themarkup.org/investigations/2025/05/20/the-nyc-algorithm-deciding-which-families-are-under-watch-for-child-abuse.

27. Ibid.

28. New York City Department of Health and Mental Hygiene, "Automated Decision Systems Annual Report," 2024.

29. Data & Society Research Institute, "Algorithmic Citizenship in the Smart City," 2023.

30. Albert Fox Cahn, "The First Effort to Regulate AI Was a Spectacular Failure," Fast Company, June 18, 2021, www.fastcompany.com/90436012/the-first-effort-to-regulate-ai-was-a-spectacular-failure; Richardson, "Confronting Black Boxes."

31. Allegheny County Department of Human Services, "Allegheny Family Screening Tool," www.alleghenycounty.us/Human-Services/News-Events/Accomplishments/Allegheny-Family-Screening-Tool.aspx

32. Marissa Gerchick et al., "The Devil is in the Details: Interrogating Values Embedded in the Allegheny Family Screening Tool," 2023 ACM Conference on Fairness, Accountability, and Transparency (FAccT '23), June 2023. The ACLU audit found the training data contained "roughly 800 variables."

33. Virginia Eubanks, "A response to Allegheny County DHS," February 16, 2018, `https://virginia-eubanks.com/2018/02/16/a-response-to-allegheny-county-dhs/`

34. Virginia Eubanks, *Automating Inequality: How High-Tech Tools Profile, Police, and Punish the Poor* (New York: St. Martin's Press, 2018), Chapter 4, "The Allegheny Algorithm."

35. Sally Ho and Garance Burke, "Child welfare algorithm faces Justice Department scrutiny," Associated Press, January 31, 2023.

36. Ibid.

37. Katherine Rittenhouse, Emily Putnam-Hornstein, and Rhema Vaithianathan, "Algorithms, Humans and Racial Disparities in Child Protective Services," 2023; ACLU and Human Rights Data Analysis Group, "The Devil is in the Details," June 2023; Neil Ballantyne, "The harm that data do: The case of the Allegheny Family Screening Tool," *Medium*, August 7, 2023.

38. Jeremy Goldhaber-Fiebert and Lea Prince, Stanford University Impact Evaluation, April 2019; Hornby Zeller Associates, "Allegheny County Predictive Risk Modeling Tool Implementation: Process Evaluation," January 2018.

39. Virginia Eubanks, "A response to Allegheny County DHS," February 16, 2018.

40. "An algorithm that screens for child neglect in Allegheny County raises concerns," WESA/ Associated Press, April 29, 2022.

41. ACLU, "How Policy Hidden in an Algorithm is Threatening Families in This Pennsylvania County," August 2, 2023.

42. Allegheny County Department of Human Services, "Summarizing Recent Research on Predictive Risk Models in Child Welfare," April 2024.

43. Princeton Gerrymandering Project, "Redistricting Report Card," `https://gerrymander.princeton.edu/redistricting-report-card/`

44. "Redistricting in N.C.: New maps approved, favoring GOP," Spectrum News, November 4, 2021.

45. Jowei Chen, University of Michigan Department of Political Science, `https://sites.lsa.umich.edu/jowei/`; See also expert reports filed in Harper v. Hall and Common Cause v. Lewis.

46. "Political stakes are high as trial begins in NC gerrymandering lawsuit," WFAE, January 4, 2022; Expert Report of Dr. Jowei Chen, Harper v. Hall, North Carolina Superior Court.

47. Princeton Gerrymandering Project analysis of North Carolina 2021 maps; "NC Republicans have drawn gerrymandered maps, but other states are considered worse," WFAE, October 29, 2021.

48. Moore v. Harper, 600 U.S. 1 (2023). The Supreme Court, in a 6-3 decision authored by Chief Justice John Roberts, rejected the "independent state legislature theory" and held that state courts may review state legislatures' congressional redistricting plans for compliance with state law. The case arose from the North Carolina redistricting litigation when Republican legislators argued that the Elections Clause gave state legislatures sole authority over federal election rules without judicial oversight.

49. Moore v. Harper, 600 U.S. ___ (2023).

50. "North Carolina Supreme Court Rehears State-Level Redistricting Case," Democracy Docket, March 14, 2023; Harper v. Hall (on rehearing), April 2023.

51. Princeton Gerrymandering Project, "Redistricting Report Card," `https://gerrymander.princeton.edu/`

52. "'Gerrymandering at its worst': Public commenters pan proposed electoral maps," NC Newsline, October 28, 2021.

53. Princeton Gerrymandering Project, "North Carolina," `https://gerrymander.princeton.edu/reforms/nc/`

54. Louis v. SafeRent Solutions, LLC, Case No. 22-cv-10800 (D. Mass.); Karlena Hamblin case documented in Erin McElroy et al., "Tenant Screening Algorithms and the Rise of Platform Urbanism," 2023.

55. Danielle Keats Citron, "Technological Due Process," Washington University Law Review 85 (2008): 1249-1313. See also Kate Crawford and Jason Schultz, "Big Data and Due Process: Toward a Framework to Redress Predictive Privacy Harms," *Boston College Law Review* 55 (2014): 93-128.

56. Deirdre K. Mulligan and Kenneth A. Bamberger, "Saving Governance-by-Design," *California Law Review* 106 (2018): 697-784. See also Ryan Calo, "Artificial Intelligence Policy: A Primer and Roadmap," *UC Davis Law Review* 51 (2017): 399-435.

57. AI Now Institute, "Algorithmic Impact Assessments: A Practical Framework for Public Agency Accountability," April 2018; AI Now Institute, "Confronting Tech Power: 2023 Landscape Report," April 2023.

58. Ibid.

59. U.S. Government Accountability Office, "Artificial Intelligence: Agencies Have Begun Implementation but Need to Complete Key Requirements," GAO-24-105980, December 2023; GAO, "Artificial Intelligence: An Accountability Framework for Federal Agencies and Other Entities," GAO-21-519SP, June 2021.

60. Algorithmic Accountability Act of 2023, S.2892, 118th Congress (2023-2024); H.R.5628, 118th Congress (2023-2024). See also Senator Ron Wyden's office summary at wyden.senate.gov.

61. European Union, "Artificial Intelligence Act," Official Journal of the European Union, 2024.

62. Ibid.

63. City of Amsterdam, "Algorithm Register: Transparency in Automated Decision-Making," 2024.

64. City of Helsinki, "AI Ethics Committee Annual Report," 2024.

65. San Francisco Board of Supervisors, "Surveillance Technology Ordinance," 2019.

66. Future of Privacy Forum, "AI Governance Behind the Scenes: Emerging Practices for AI Impact Assessments," December 2024; Future of Privacy Forum, "U.S. State AI Legislation" report, September 2024.

67. Brookings Institution Artificial Intelligence and Emerging Technology Initiative reports, available at brookings.edu/projects/artificial-intelligence-and-emerging-technology-initiative/; Darrell M. West and John R. Allen, "Turning Point: Policymaking in the Era of Artificial Intelligence," Brookings Institution Press, 2020.

68. Sarah Williams and MIT Civic Data Design Lab, research on AI in city government, discussed in MIT Technology Review, "How AI can make city government work better for residents," June 2025; MIT GOV/LAB, "Generative AI for Pro-Democracy Platforms," March 2024.

69. Center for Democracy and Technology, AI Policy and Governance program publications, available at cdt.org/area-of-focus/ai-policy-governance/; CDT, "AI Action Plan Should Promote AI Transparency, Accuracy, Effectiveness and Reliability," March 2025.

70. Data & Society Research Institute, "Assembling Accountability: Algorithmic Impact Assessment for the Public Interest," 2021; Data & Society Algorithmic Impact Methods Lab (AIMLab) research, available at datasociety.net/research/ai-on-the-ground/.

71. AI Now Institute, Ada Lovelace Institute, and Open Government Partnership, "Algorithmic Accountability for the Public Sector," 2021 (updated 2025); AI Now Institute, "Algorithmic Impact Assessments: A Practical Framework for Public Agency Accountability," April 2018.

Chapter 4

1. The initial $17.3M settlement was proposed in 2019 but rejected by the 9th Circuit in 2021. A revised $5.2M settlement was also rejected in December 2023.

2. Lisa Kim v. Match Group Inc., Tinder age discrimination settlement, $17.3 million, 2024. Lowe & Associates, "Tinder Ordered to Pay $17.3 Million to Class Members to Settle Claims for Age Discrimination," May 21, 2024.

3. Tim Giordano quoted in Jacobin, "Dating App Giant Match Group Is Being Sued for Conning Users," February 2025.

4. Megan Cerullo, "Tinder and Hinge Dating Apps are Designed to Addict Users, Lawsuit Claims," CBS News, February 15, 2024; NPR, "Maker of Tinder, Hinge sued over 'addictive' dating apps that put profits over love," February 15, 2024.

5. Rebecca Barker, "Match Group, Owner of Hinge, Tinder, and the League, Sued for Predatory Business Model," Inc., February 21, 2024.

6. Oksayan v. Match Group Inc., 3:24-cv-00888 (U.S. 2024).

7. Paubox, "Real-world examples of healthcare AI bias," May 11, 2025.

8. Ziad Obermeyer et al., "Dissecting racial bias in an algorithm used to manage the health of populations," *Science*, October 25, 2019.

9. Kadija Ferryman, Johns Hopkins Bloomberg School of Public Health, "Rooting Out AI's Biases," *Hopkins Bloomberg Public Health Magazine*, 2023.

10. PMC, "Addressing bias in big data and AI for health care: A call for open science," October 2021.

11. Maples, Bethanie, Merve Cerit, Aditya Vishwanath, and Roy Pea. "Loneliness and suicide mitigation for students using GPT3-enabled chatbots." *npj mental health research* 3, no. 1 (2024): 4.

12. Character.AI litigation following 14-year-old's suicide, Florida mother lawsuit, October 2024; CNN Business, "Senators demand information from AI companion apps in the wake of kids' safety concerns, lawsuits," April 3, 2025.

13. Harvard Business School Working Paper 25-018, "Lessons From an App Update at Replika AI: Identity," 2025; Gavin Bridge, "AI Chatbot Credited With Preventing Suicide. Should It Be?" 404 Media, May 20, 2024.

14. CNN Business, "Senators demand information from AI companion apps in the wake of kids' safety concerns, lawsuits," April 3, 2025.

15. Baillifard et al., "Implementing Learning Principles with a Personal AI Tutor: A Case Study," arXiv:2309.13060, September 10, 2023.

16. Baillifard et al., "Effective learning with a personal AI tutor: A case study," *Education and Information Technologies,* Vol. 30, pages 297-312, July 13, 2024.

17. Wikipedia, "Algorithmic radicalization," documenting Austrian cases of teenagers radicalized via TikTok: early 2023 LGBTQ pride parade plot and 2024 Taylor Swift concert plot in Vienna.

18. Fung Institute, Berkeley, "Op-Ed: Social media algorithms & their effects on American politics," May 2, 2022, documenting TikTok study showing rapid radicalization within two hours of engagement with transphobic content.

19. Whittaker et al., "Recommender systems and the amplification of extremist content," *Internet Policy Review,* June 30, 2021; UK Government Online Harms White Paper, 2019; UK Commission for Countering Extremism report, 2019; EU Counter-Terrorism Coordinator report, Council of the European Union, 2020.

20. NPR, "New study shows just how Facebook's algorithm shapes conservative and liberal bubbles," July 27, 2023; documentation of 2020 election and January 6th Capitol insurrection connection to Facebook's "Stop the Steal" groups.

Chapter 5

1. Derek Mobley v. Workday, Inc., Case No. 3:23-cv-00770-RFL (N.D. Cal. filed Feb. 1, 2023); Daniel Wiessner, "Workday accused of facilitating widespread bias in novel AI lawsuit," Reuters, February 21, 2024.

2. Ibid.; "Mobley v. Workday: Amended Complaint Highlights Discrimination and AI Bias in Employment Screening," Holistic AI, February 20, 2024, `www.holisticai.com/news/workday-lawsuit-amended-complaint`.

3. Derek Mobley v. Workday, Inc., First Amended Complaint, Case No. 3:23-cv-00770-RFL (N.D. Cal. filed Feb. 20, 2024).

4. Mobley v. Workday, Inc., 740 F.Supp.3d 796 (N.D. Cal. July 12, 2024); Joseph O'Keefe, Evandro Gigante, and Hannah Morris, "Mobley v. Workday: Court Holds AI Service Providers Could Be Directly Liable for Employment Discrimination Under 'Agent' Theory," Seyfarth Shaw LLP, July 15, 2024.

5. U.S. Equal Employment Opportunity Commission, "Amicus Brief in Support of Plaintiff," Mobley v. Workday, Inc., Case No. 3:23-cv-00770-RFL (N.D. Cal. filed April 9, 2024).

6. "AI Bias Lawsuit Against Workday Reaches Next Stage as Court Grants Conditional Certification of ADEA Claim," Law and the Workplace, June 11, 2025, `www.lawandtheworkplace.com/2025/06/ai-bias-lawsuit-against-workday`.

7. Jeremy Gorner, "Chicago Police Use 'Heat List' as Strategy to Prevent Violence," *Chicago Tribune,* August 21, 2013; Aaron Tucek, "Constraining Big Brother: The Legal Deficiencies Surrounding Chicago's Use of the Strategic Subject List," University of Chicago Legal Forum, vol. 2018 (2019): Article 18.

8. Gorner, "Chicago Police Use 'Heat List'"; Matt Stroud, "The Minority Report: Chicago's New Police Computer Predicts Crimes, But Is It Racist?" *The Verge,* February 19, 2014.

9. "How Predictive Policing Got A Chicago Man Shot Twice," Techdirt, June 3, 2021, `www.techdirt.com/2021/06/03/how-predictive-policing-got-chicago-man-shot-twice/`; "Predictive policing

makes Robert McDaniel criminal target," AIAAIC Repository, www.aiaaic.org/aiaaic-repository/predictive-policing-makes-robert-mcdaniel-criminal-target.

10. Jessica Saunders, Priscillia Hunt, and John S. Hollywood, "Predictions put into practice: a quasi-experimental evaluation of Chicago's predictive policing pilot," Journal of Experimental Criminology, vol. 12, no. 3 (2016): 347-371; Yana Kunichoff and Patrick Sier, "Study Casts Doubt on Chicago Police's Secretive 'Heat List,'" Chicago Magazine, August 19, 2016.

11. Chicago Police Department, "Strategic Subject List – Dashboard," Chicago Data Portal, https://data.cityofchicago.org/4aki-r3np (accessed December 7, 2017); Tucek, "Constraining Big Brother," at 531-533.

12. Frank Main, "What Gets People on Watch List? Chicago Police Fought to Keep Secret," Chicago Sun-Times, May 18, 2017; Tucek, "Constraining Big Brother," at 544-547.

13. Steve Stecklow, "Why Facebook Is Losing the War on Hate Speech in Myanmar," Reuters, August 15, 2018, www.reuters.com/investigates/special-report/myanmar-facebook-hate/.

14. Sheera Frenkel and Cecilia Kang, "Inside Facebook's Data Wars," *The New York Times,* July 14, 2021; Daniel Funke and Daniela Flamini, "A Guide to Anti-Misinformation Actions Around the World," Poynter Institute, August 2018.

15. UN Human Rights Council, "Report of the Independent International Fact-Finding Mission on Myanmar," A/HRC/39/64, September 12, 2018, paras. 73-75.

16. Karen Hao and Deepa Seetharaman, "How Facebook Got Addicted to Spreading Misinformation," *Wall Street Journal,* October 25, 2021; Kate Klonick, "The Facebook Oversight Board: Creating an Independent Institution to Adjudicate Online Free Expression," *Yale Law Journal,* vol. 129 (2020): 2418-2499.

17. Abdi Latif Dahir and Hannah Beech, "As War Rips Apart Ethiopia, Social Media Fuels Atrocities," *The New York Times,* December 15, 2021; Hallelujah Lulie Tesfaye, "Overselling AI: Facebook's Content Moderation Issues in Ethiopia," Annenberg School for Communication, University of Pennsylvania, 2022.

18. Global Witness and Foxglove, "Facebook Approves Hate Speech Ads in Ethiopia Amid Conflict," November 2021, `www.globalwitness.org/en/campaigns/digital-threats/facebook-approves-hate-speech-ads-ethiopia-amid-conflict/`.

19. Brooke Erin Duffy and Colten Meisner, "How aspiring influencers are forced to fight the algorithm," *MIT Technology Review,* July 14, 2022, `www.technologyreview.com/2022/07/14/1055906/tiktok-influencers-moderation-bias/`; Carolina Are, "'Dysfunctional' appeals and failures of algorithmic justice in Instagram and TikTok content moderation," Information, Communication & Society (2024): 1997-2014.

20. Equal Employment Opportunity Commission v. iTutorGroup, Inc., Case No. 1:22-cv-2565 (E.D.N.Y. filed May 5, 2022); "EEOC Settles First AI-Discrimination Lawsuit," Sullivan & Cromwell LLP, August 2023.

21. EEOC v. iTutorGroup, Inc., Complaint, Case No. 1:22-cv-2565 (E.D.N.Y. filed May 5, 2022), paras. 15-20.

22. EEOC v. iTutorGroup, Inc., Consent Decree, Case No. 1:22-cv-2565 (E.D.N.Y. filed Aug. 9, 2023); "EEOC Secures First Workplace Artificial Intelligence Settlement," Greenberg Traurig LLP, August 9, 2023.

23. Kyra Wilson and Aylin Caliskan, "AI tools show biases in ranking job applicants' names according to perceived race and gender," *University of Washington News,* October 31, 2024, `www.washington.edu/news/2024/10/31/ai-bias-resume-screening-race-gender/`.

24. New York City Council, "Local Law 144 of 2021," December 11, 2021, codified as NYC Admin. Code § 20-870 et seq.

25. New York City Department of Consumer and Worker Protection, "Automated Employment Decision Tools," Final Rules, April 6, 2023.

26. Julia Stoyanovich et al., "Null Compliance: NYC Local Law 144 and the Challenges of Algorithm Accountability," Proceedings of the 2024 ACM Conference on Fairness, Accountability, and Transparency (2024): 1893-1905.

27. Riana Pfefferkorn et al., "New Research: NYC Algorithmic Transparency Law Is Falling Short of Its Goals," *Consumer Reports,* February 8, 2024.

28. Solon Barocas et al., "Auditing Work: Exploring the New York City Algorithmic Bias Audit Regime," Proceedings of the 2024 ACM Conference on Fairness, Accountability, and Transparency (2024): 1881-1892.

29. Ibid., at 1886-1888.

30. Emanuel Moss et al., "Comments on Proposed Rules Related to Automated Employment Decision Tools," New York City Department of Consumer and Worker Protection, February 4, 2023.

Chapter 6

1. Lucas Wright, Roxana Mika Muenster, Briana Vecchione, et al., "Null Compliance: NYC Local Law 144 and the Challenges of Algorithm Accountability," in *Proceedings of the 2024 ACM Conference on Fairness, Accountability, and Transparency* (Rio de Janeiro, Brazil: ACM, 2024), `https://doi.org/10.1145/3630106.3658998`.

2. Lara Groves, Jacob Metcalf, Alayna Kennedy, Briana Vecchione, and Andrew Strait, "Auditing Work: Exploring the New York City Algorithmic Bias Audit Regime," in Proceedings of the 2024 ACM Conference on Fairness, Accountability, and Transparency (Rio de Janeiro, Brazil: ACM, 2024), `https://doi.org/10.1145/3630106.3658959`.

3. "Amsterdam and Helsinki Launch Algorithm Registries to Bring Transparency to Public Deployments of AI," *VentureBeat*, September 28, 2020, https://venturebeat.com/ai/amsterdam-and-helsinki-launch-algorithm-registries.

4. "Standard Launched to Help Cities Open Up About Algorithms," *Eurocities Public Buyers Community*, accessed November 1, 2025, https://public-buyers-community.ec.europa.eu/news/standard-launched-help-cities-open-about-algorithms.

5. "Inside Amsterdam's High-Stakes Experiment to Create Fair Welfare AI," *MIT Technology Review,* July 30, 2025, www.technologyreview.com/2025/06/11/1118233/amsterdam-fair-welfare-ai.

6. Min Kyung Lee, Daniel Kusbit, Anson Kahng, et al., "WeBuildAI: Participatory Framework for Algorithmic Governance," Proceedings of the ACM on Human-Computer Interaction 3, no. CSCW (November 2019): 1-35, https://doi.org/10.1145/3359283.

7. "From Margins to the Table: Charting the Potential for Public Participatory Governance of Algorithmic Decision Making," in Proceedings of the 2025 ACM Conference on Fairness, Accountability, and Transparency (2025), https://dl.acm.org/doi/10.1145/3715275.3732173.

8. Lauren Kirchner, "Can Algorithms Violate Fair Housing Laws?," The Markup, September 24, 2020, https://themarkup.org/locked-out/2020/09/24/fair-housing-laws-algorithms-tenant-screenings.

9. "Screened Out: How Faulty Algorithms Are Shutting Doors on Fair Housing," *American University Business Law Review,* September 24, 2024, https://aublr.org/2024/09/screened-out-how-faulty-algorithms-are-shutting-doors.

10. U.S. Department of Housing and Urban Development, "HUD Issues Fair Housing Act Guidance on Applications of Artificial Intelligence," press release, May 2023, www.hud.gov/press/press_releases_media_advisories/hud_no_24_098.

11. "How a Computer Algorithm Caused a Grading Crisis in British Schools," CNBC, August 21, 2020, www.cnbc.com/2020/08/21/computer-algorithm-caused-a-grading-crisis-in-british-schools.html.

12. Angela Kelly, "A Tale of Two Algorithms: The Appeal and Repeal of Calculated Grades Systems in England and Ireland in 2020," *British Educational Research Journal* 47, no. 6 (February 2021): 1234-1258, https://doi.org/10.1002/berj.3705.

13. "'F**k the Algorithm': What the World Can Learn from the UK's A-level Grading Fiasco," *LSE Impact Blog,* August 26, 2020, https://blogs.lse.ac.uk/impactofsocialsciences/2020/08/26/fk-the-algorithm.

14. Lucile Ter-Minassian, "Democratizing AI Governance: Balancing Expertise and Public Participation," arXiv preprint arXiv:2502.08651 (2025), https://arxiv.org/abs/2502.08651.

15. "AI Needs Safeguards to Prevent Democratic Erosion," Schwartz Reisman Institute for Technology and Society, University of Toronto, https://srinstitute.utoronto.ca/democracy-rewired.

Chapter 7

1. Dastin, Jeffrey. "Amazon Scraps Secret AI Recruiting Tool That Showed Bias Against Women." Reuters, October 10, 2018. www.reuters.com/article/us-amazon-com-jobs-automation-insight-idUSKCN1MK08G
2. "Amazon Ditched AI Recruitment Software Because It Was Biased Against Women." *MIT Technology Review*, October 10, 2018. www.technologyreview.com/2018/10/10/139858/amazon-ditched-ai-recruitment-software-because-it-was-biased-against-women/
3. Kannan, P.K. "The Problem With Amazon's AI Recruiter." *Robert H. Smith School of Business*, University of Maryland. www.rhsmith.umd.edu/research/problem-amazons-ai-recruiter
4. Hu, W. "Unilever's Practice on AI-based Recruitment." Research Paper, August 2, 2023. www.researchgate.net/publication/373763740_Unilever's_Practice_on_AI-based_Recruitment
5. "Next Gen AI in Action: Unilever's AI-Powered Recruitment Revolution." GSD Council, March 9, 2021. www.gsdcouncil.org/blogs/next-gen-ai-in-action-unilever-s-ai-powered-recruitment-revolution

6. Farzaneh, N., et al. "Collaborative Strategies for Deploying AI-Based Physician Decision Support Systems: Challenges and Deployment Approaches." npj Digital Medicine 6, 137 (2023). www.nature.com/articles/s41746-023-00889-6

7. Goh, E., et al. "Physician Clinical Decision Modification and Bias Assessment in a Randomized Controlled Trial of AI Assistance." Communications Medicine, March 4, 2025. www.nature.com/articles/s43856-025-00781-2

8. Spiekermann, Sarah. "What to Expect From IEEE 7000: The First Standard for Building Ethical Systems." IEEE Technology and Society, February 21, 2022. technologyandsociety.org/what-to-expect-from-ieee-7000-the-first-standard-for-building-ethical-systems/

9. "IEEE Launches New Standard to Address Ethical Concerns During Systems Design." IEEE Standards Association, September 15, 2021. https://standards.ieee.org/news/ieee-7000/

10. "Ethics and Society Newsletter #1." Hugging Face, 2020. https://huggingface.co/blog/ethics-soc-1

11. "Ethics and Society Newsletter #5: Hugging Face Goes To Washington and Other Summer 2023 Musings." *Hugging Face*. https://huggingface.co/blog/ethics-soc-5

12. Ibid.

13. "Oversight Board (Meta)." Wikipedia, accessed November 2025. https://en.wikipedia.org/wiki/Oversight_Board_(Meta)

14. Ang, Peng Hwa and Haristya, Sherly. "The Governance, Legitimacy and Efficacy of Facebook's Oversight Board: A Model for Global Tech Platforms?" SAGE Journals, 2024. https://journals.sagepub.com/doi/full/10.1177/27523543241266860

15. "Meta's Oversight Board Needs Access to Facebook's Algorithms to Do Its Job." Brennan Center for Justice. www.brennancenter.org/our-work/analysis-opinion/metas-oversight-board-needs-access-facebooks-algorithms-do-its-job

16. Association for Computing Machinery. "ACM Code of Ethics and Professional Conduct," updated 2018. www.acm.org/code-of-ethics

17. Boards Increasingly Tout AI Expertise." Corporate Compliance Insights, August 1, 2025. www.corporatecomplianceinsights.com/news-roundup-august-1-2025/

18. Wynants, S., Childers, G., De La Torre Roman, Y., Budar-Turner, D., & Vasquez, P. (2025). "ETHICAL Principles AI Framework for Higher Education." California State University, Fullerton. https://genai.calstate.edu/communities/faculty/ethical-and-responsible-use-ai/ethical-principles-ai-framework-higher-education

19. "What role should higher education institutions play in fostering AI ethics? Insights from science and engineering graduate students." *International Journal of STEM Education,* October 2, 2025. https://stemeducationjournal.springeropen.com/articles/10.1186/s40594-025-00567-x

20. "AI Ethics in Higher Education: How Schools Are Proceeding." *EdTech Magazine,* June 10, 2025. https://edtechmagazine.com/higher/article/2025/06/ai-ethics-higher-education-how-schools-are-proceeding-perfcon

21. Association for Computing Machinery. "ACM Code of Ethics and Professional Conduct," updated 2018. www.acm.org/code-of-ethics

22. "AI Governance Frameworks: Guide to Ethical AI Implementation." Consilien. https://consilien.com/news/ai-governance-frameworks-guide-to-ethical-ai-implementation

23. Saxena, D., Kahn, Z., Moon, E. S., et al. (2025). "Emerging Practices in Participatory AI Design in Public Sector Innovation." CHI EA '25, April 26-May 1, 2025. https://arxiv.org/html/2502.18689v1

24. Ibid.

25. Rice, B. T., Rasmus, S., Onders, R., Thomas, T., et al. (2025). "Community-engaged artificial intelligence: an upstream, participatory design, development, testing, validation, use and monitoring framework for artificial intelligence and machine learning models in the Alaska Tribal Health System." Frontiers in Artificial Intelligence, March 21, 2025. www.frontiersin.org/journals/artificial-intelligence/articles/10.3389/frai.2025.1568886/full

26. "Why corporate integrity is key to shaping future use of AI." World Economic Forum, October 2024. www.weforum.org/stories/2024/10/corporate-integrity-future-ai-regulation/

27. Ibid.

28. "AI in Focus in 2025: Boards and Shareholders Set Their Sights on AI." Harvard Law School Forum on Corporate Governance, April 2, 2025. https://corpgov.law.harvard.edu/2025/04/02/ai-in-focus-in-2025-boards-and-shareholders-set-their-sights-on-ai/

29. "Why corporate integrity is key to shaping future use of AI." World Economic Forum, October 2024.

30. Ibid.

31. "AI in Focus in 2025: Boards and Shareholders Set Their Sights on AI." Harvard Law School Forum on Corporate Governance, April 2, 2025.

Chapter 8

1. Open Communities v. Harbor Group Management, consent decree, U.S. District Court for the Northern District of Illinois, 2024. See also Patrick Sisson, "What's Next for Heavily Scrutinized Multifamily Tenant Screening Tools?" *Propmodo*, January 17, 2025, `https://propmodo.com/whats-next-for-heavily-scrutinized-multifamily-tenant-screening-tools/`

2. Patrick Sisson, "AI is used to discriminate against renters, a Chicago-area housing group says in lawsuit," WBEZ Chicago, October 5, 2023, `www.wbez.org/race-class-communities/2023/10/05/housing-lawsuit-alleges-ai-discrimination`

3. Alicia Adamczyk, "This Man Changed His Name from José to Joe and Suddenly Started Getting More Callbacks," *Business Insider*, September 2014; "José vs. Joe: Who Gets a Callback?" BuzzFeed Video, September 2014.

4. Marianne Bertrand and Sendhil Mullainathan, "Are Emily and Greg More Employable Than Lakisha and Jamal? A Field Experiment on Labor Market Discrimination," *American Economic Review* 94, no. 4 (2004): 991–1013.

5. Kyra Wilson et al., "Gender, Race, and Intersectional Bias in AI Resume Screening via Language Model Retrieval," Proceedings of the AAAI/ACM Conference on AI, Ethics, and Society (October 2024).

6. University of Washington News, "AI Tools Show Biases in Ranking Job Applicants' Names According to Perceived Race and Gender," October 31, 2024.

7. Emma van Inwegen et al., "The Impact of AI Writing Assistance on Labor Market Outcomes," MIT Sloan School of Management Working Paper, 2023. Note: This study examined AI writing assistance (grammar and spelling improvement), not ATS optimization tools.

8. Emma van Inwegen, Zanele Munyikwa, and John J. Horton, "Algorithmic Writing Assistance on Jobseekers' Resumes Increases Hires," MIT Sloan School of Management working paper, April 26, 2023, `https://mitsloan.mit.edu/ideas-made-to-matter/job-seekers-ai-boosted-resumes-more-likely-to-be-hired`

9. Connecticut Fair Housing Center, "Center Files Federal Lawsuit Against National Tenant Screening Company," April 24, 2018.

10. National Housing Law Project, "Arroyo v. CoreLogic," July 31, 2018.

11. Cohen Milstein Sellers & Toll PLLC, "Connecticut Fair Housing Center, et al. v. CoreLogic Rental Property Solutions," Case No. 3:18-cv-00705 (D. Conn.).

12. U.S. Department of Housing and Urban Development, "Guidance on Application of Fair Housing Standards to the Use of Criminal Records by Providers of Housing," April 2016.

13. U.S. Government Accountability Office, "Rental Housing: Use and Federal Oversight of Property Technology," GAO-25-107196, July 10, 2025.

14. Ibid. The report details enforcement actions by DOJ, FTC, CFPB, and HUD against property technology companies including CoreLogic, AppFolio, and RealPage.

15. Change.org, "Remove Proctortrack from Western University," 2020 (petition gathered over 10,000 signatures).

16. Western University communications regarding proctoring software transition, May 2021.

17. *Christian Science Monitor,* "Online Exams Raise Concerns of Racial Bias in Facial Recognition," November 17, 2020.

18. VICE Motherboard, "Proctorio Is Using Racist Algorithms to Detect Faces," April 8, 2021; Akash Satheesan's technical analysis validated by independent security researchers.

19. Shea Swauger, "Software That Monitors Students During Tests Perpetuates Inequality and Violates Their Privacy," *MIT Technology Review,* August 7, 2020.

20. "AI in the Living Room: The Problem with Online Exam Proctors," Lutzker & Lutzker LLP, July 1, 2021, `www.lutzker.com/ai-in-the-living-room-the-problem-with-online-exam-proctors/`

21. New York City Department of Consumer and Worker Protection, Local Law 144 of 2021 (Automated Employment Decision Tools), enforcement effective July 5, 2023.

22. Kyra Wilson et al., "Gender, Race, and Intersectional Bias in AI Resume Screening," *AAAI/ACM Conference on AI, Ethics, and Society,* October 2024.

23. UN Office of the High Commissioner for Human Rights, "Landmark Ruling by Dutch Court Stops Government Attempts to Spy on the Poor – UN Expert," February 5, 2020.

24. Hague District Court, NJCM et al. v. The State of the Netherlands, Case No. C/09/550982/HA ZA 18/388, February 5, 2020.

25. Philip Alston, Report of the Special Rapporteur on Extreme Poverty and Human Rights on Digital Welfare States, A/74/493, United Nations General Assembly, October 2019.

26. Amnesty International, "Xenophobic Machines: Discrimination Through Unregulated Use of Algorithms in the Dutch Childcare Benefits Scandal," October 2021.

27. BMC Medical Informatics and Decision Making, review of AI in healthcare decision-making, 2024.

28. See generally, AI ethics guidelines from American Medical Association and other medical professional organizations on human oversight requirements for clinical AI systems.

29. Journal of Medical Internet Research, studies on AI-assisted shared decision-making in healthcare, 2023-2024.

30. Jayakumar et al., "Application of Artificial Intelligence in Shared Decision Making: Scoping Review," *Journal of Medical Internet Research,* August 2022, `https://pmc.ncbi.nlm.nih.gov/articles/PMC9399841/`

31. For a comprehensive discussion of these regulatory frameworks, see Chapter 6, "Democratic AI Governance," of this volume.

32. Patrick Sisson, "What's Next for Heavily Scrutinized Multifamily Tenant Screening Tools?" *Propmodo,* January 17, 2025, `https://propmodo.com/whats-next-for-heavily-scrutinized-multifamily-tenant-screening-tools/`

Index

C. Shah, *Agent Nation*, https://doi.org/10.1007/979-8-8688-2454-8

B

C

D

E

F

G

H

I

J

K

L

M

N

O

P, Q

Y, Z

GPSR Compliance

The European Union's (EU) General Product Safety Regulation (GPSR) is a set of rules that requires consumer products to be safe and our obligations to ensure this.

If you have any concerns about our products, you can contact us on ProductSafety@springernature.com

In case Publisher is established outside the EU, the EU authorized representative is:

Springer Nature Customer Service Center GmbH
Europaplatz 3
69115 Heidelberg, Germany

Batch number: 10214176

Printed by Printforce, the Netherlands